How to Start a Freight Brokerage Company

Quickly Learn the Ins and Outs of the Business and Set Yourself Up for Success

Colton Ryder

sources. Please consult a licensed professional before attempting any techniques outlined in this book.

By reading this document, the reader agrees that under no circumstances is the author responsible for any losses, direct or indirect, which are incurred as a result of the use of information contained within this document, including, but not limited to, — errors, omissions, or inaccuracies.

Table of Contents

Introduction

The current statistics of unemployment across the world is steadily rising. The primary reason for the increase in this number is due to the shortage of jobs.

However, thanks to technology, the world has now become a global village making it possible for other industries to grow and expand, creating job opportunities that did not seem possible over the years. One such sector is the freight-forwarding sector.

The export and import industry is a lucrative business; it does, however, become quite expensive to transport goods from one country to another if you do not know what steps to follow.

This is why people across the world prefer using freight forwarding companies. This book will discuss an essential business in the freight-forwarding sector: the freight brokerage business.

We will discuss and highlight the basics of a freight brokerage business and the benefits of starting one. We will also look at the necessary steps you need to follow as well as how to set it up in the right way.

Other things this book will highlight are the problems people face while in this business and I will provide solutions to help you overcome these challenges. For those already in the industry, we will also discuss strategies that can help you scale up your business from what you are currently earning to a multiple six and seven figure business. Also, we'll discuss how you can negotiate your way to a thriving business.

So, who is this book for?

- Anyone who wants to learn how to become a successful freight broker.

- Anyone who wants to know how to advance their freight brokerage business earnings.

- Anyone who wants to have an in-depth knowledge of the freight brokerage business.

- Anyone who desires to become a freight broker.

- Anyone who wants to learn various strategies to overcome the challenges in the freight brokerage business.

- Anyone who wants to learn the advantages of the freight brokerage business.

Before we take an in-depth look into the freight brokerage business; it is essential for us to lay a foundation by understanding what it is all about. We will therefore, take a closer look at the freight transport business.

The Freight Transport Industry

The freight transport industry deals with the transportation of merchandise goods, commodities, and cargo. This transportation industry is commonly referenced as shipping primarily because the first common form of goods transportation from one state to another was done by sea.

However, this mode of shipping has diversified and led to the inclusion of other modes of transportation that are quite effective.

Modes of freight transportation

The different modes of freight transportation include:

Ship

Actual ships do most of the exports and imports across the world. The countries that majorly rely on ships to transport their cargo have a fleet of ships and crewmembers responsible for the transportation of the cargo. The fleet of a ship a country owns is commonly referred to as a merchant marine or the merchant navy. With the growth of the export and import industry, merchant shipping has become the lifeblood of our world's economy, as it carries approximately 90% of the world's trade with over 102,194 commercial ships working in the freight transportation industry.

Air

Air transportation has slowly become a popular means of transportation for the freight industry. Cargo transported by air is placed in specialized cargo aircraft as well as in luggage compartments in passenger aircraft. Unlike other modes of freight transportation, it is the fastest and the most expensive means of freight transportation.

Ground

Ground or land shipping is done by either a train or truck. The use of ground transportation is for the purpose of transporting cargo, merchandise goods, and commodities that arrive through the sea or by air. Transportation companies pick the commodities from the seaport or airport and transport them to their required destination. Ground transportation has made it possible for countries with limited coastlines to never worry about production facilities close to their ports.

Intermodal

The intermodal form of transportation refers to the shipment of goods that require more than one mode of transportation. This mode of transportation primarily refers to the utilization of intermodal shipping containers, which are easy to transfer between plane, ship, rail, and truck. Manufacturers use intermodal transportation to deliver goods right at the recipient's door.

How it works

The freight industry comprises of various companies that perform different functions all with the purpose of delivering cargo right at the recipient's door. The main function of the freight company is to arrange all the essential details required by the cargo transport between the carrier and the shipper.

The freight company will act as an intermediary between carrier and shipper and this helps in taking off the problems that the two parties would have experienced when working alone.

People interested in shipping an item often have a hard time locating good carriers while carriers have a difficult time finding clients. The freight company is able to use its data list making the search easier for the shipper and gives carriers reliable clients. Once the freight company sets up any shipment, they acquire a commission.

However, a freight company would not be successful were it not for the help of individuals responsible for the success of every shipment made. These individuals are known as freight brokers and freight forwarders. They are responsible for the profit a freight company makes. They also help find shippers and carriers on behalf of the company. We will discuss more about freight brokers in chapter one.

This book will help you discover and learn about the freight brokerage business and give you the courage to start one. So, let's dive in.

Chapter One: Why You Should

Start a Freight Brokerage Business

In this chapter, we will discuss who a freight broker is and the difference between a freight forwarder and a freight agent. We will also look at how a freight brokerage business works and how you can make money from this business. We will also take an in-depth look at the various misconceptions that surround this business and break them down by including facts. Finally, we will also look at the advantages of a freight brokerage business as compared to other businesses.

Who is a freight broker?

A freight broker is an individual or a company that acts as a liaison between asset carriers and shippers. You can also define freight brokers as liaisons between transport carriers and shipping requirements.

These individuals or companies simply act as middlemen between the transporter and the manufacturer and this ensures that the product arrives at its destination. The freight broker deals with the shipper and transport carrier ensuring they communicate and the cargo is transported efficiently.

However, in the freight transportation industry, other

individuals or companies also ensure the successful delivery of the merchandise goods. Like I mentioned earlier in the introduction, apart from a freight broker, there is also a freight forwarder and a freight agent.

Which begs the question, what is the difference between a freight forwarder and a freight broker? What are the similarities and differences between the two? Learning the differences between these three freight businesses makes it easier to identify the responsibilities of a freight broker without mixing up the other responsibilities.

Differences among a freight broker, a freight forwarder, and a freight agent.

The significant differences among a freight broker, a freight forwarder, and a freight agent are in the responsibilities of each party. However, before we dive into the differences of each role, it is essential to note that each of these companies plays a significant role in the freight transportation industry, as they act as intermediaries. Despite their similarities, each freight intermediary has different technical and legal obligations.

Responsibilities of a freight forwarder

A freight forwarder is an individual or a company that secures business for various importers and exporters. They also have the ability and the facility to:

- Store the cargo belonging to their clients in their warehouses. This is usually done by big forwarding businesses with their own warehouses.

- Arrange forwarding or distribution of cargo, and this is done as per their client's instructions. Delivery of freight could be in various routings or regular routings.

- Negotiate the freight rates. They communicate with shipping lines, and this helps both parties come up with a freight rate that covers their clients' interests.

- Book their clients' cargo with freight transportation as per the client's requirements.

- Prepare landing bills and negotiation/associated shipping documents.

- Issue an approved house bill wherever applicable.

- Sometimes do customs clearance on behalf of their clients.

- May or may not be qualified to ports or customs. If a freight forwarder is not accredited, they are not able to do customs clearance for their customers.

Responsibilities of a Freight Broker

A freight broker is an individual or a company responsible for:

- Arranging the transportation of merchandise goods or cargo whether via road, rail, sea, or air on behalf of the freight forwarder, consignee, or shipper.

- Connecting the cargo owner and shipping company. This earns the freight broker a commission.

- Outsourcing all freight transportation activities such as insurance, transport, etc.

- Unlike freight forwarders, freight brokers do not own company landing bills.

Other responsibilities freight brokers have include the assessment of shipper's credit, paying motor carriers, collecting receivables, and invoicing shippers among others.

Responsibilities of a freight agent

Freight agents are responsible for:

- The estimation of postal/freight rates and the recording of shipment weights and costs

- Keeping records of every good shipped, stored, and received.

- Entering the shipping information of a customer's cargo into a computer.

- Checking import and export documents to determine the customer's cargo content. They later use the tariff coding system, and this helps them classify each good accordingly.

- Preparing manifests on behalf of their customers and transmitting that data to the various cargo destinations.

Unlike a freight broker and a freight forwarder, the responsibilities of a freight agent are more customer-focused. Freight agents also work under licensed freight brokers.

However, despite the significant differences between these three freight jobs, each company or individual has to work closely together with the other entity to ensure the successful transportation of their client's goods.

A freight brokerage business cannot work independently, and it requires the help of a freight forwarder, as well as the help of a freight agent to run smoothly.

How does a freight brokerage business work?

Just like a freight broker, a freight brokerage business' main function is to connect manufacturing companies or shippers with carriers to ensure that goods arrive safely to their destinations. Understanding how the freight brokerage business works will help you understand the relationship between a freight broker, a shipper, and a carrier. Here is a step-by-step process of how the freight brokerage business works.

- *Order tender:* The first step of this process starts when a business (shipper) emailing or calling a freight broker for pickup. The freight broker then goes ahead and acquires all the necessary information they require when tendering the freight. The info the shipper provides helps the freight broker determine whether the cargo is a special order or a regularly scheduled shipment.

In addition to the shipment information, they also inquire about the delivery location of the freight and the contact information. They also need to know whether the freight has special handling and packaging instructions, the equipment, the freight's compliance standards, and the consignee's preference.

- *Freight Scheduling:* Once the freight broker has obtained the relevant information about the freight, the next step is to enter the freight order into the freight management system. This system enables freight brokers to schedule and confirm the exact date the order needs to be picked up and delivered.

This is the stage where the services of a freight broker are most valuable. They take time to secure the necessary transportation by selling and booking a professional carrier for the order. Freight brokers build networks with vetted carriers, and they end up forming long-lasting relationships with reliable carriers.

The freight scheduling stage is also where the carrier shares important handling information with the freight broker. Before booking a carrier, the freight broker has to confirm whether the carrier has

  o Appropriate equipment that is up to date and clean

  o A current and valid license

  o The required number of cargo and a liability insurance cover

  o Ability to handle special needs like team transit, and driver assist among others

- A trailer that will not carry any potential contaminants

- Commitment to the delivery time

- *Dispatch:* Once the freight scheduling process is complete, the next step is the dispatch stage. When the time finally comes for the freight to be picked up, the freight broker connects with the carrier, double checks all the essential information like the name, cell phone number, trailer type, and the current location of the carrier. The freight broker also recommunicates the handling requirements of the freight and later gives the carrier the pick-up information.

- *Loading:* The freight broker stays in touch with the carrier during the entire loading process. The loading process is not considered complete until the cargo is placed on the trailer. The trailer is then shut or sealed, and then the carrier signs the shipper's Bill of Landing. Signing the bill means that the carrier accepts liability and possession of the freight.

When communicating with the carrier, the freight broker verifies the case count and skid. They also verify whether the carrier is carrying the right freight and the destination of the freight as shown on the bill. This step is necessary as it prevents the loading of the wrong products, and can derail the delivery time of the goods, leading to unnecessary stress to the shipper and the freight broker.

- *Transit:* The freight broker stays in contact with the carrier throughout the transportation of the freight. They use technology like a GPS tracker to track the progress of the cargo and maintain the location of the freight during the transportation stage. Freight brokers also make regular calls to the carriers during the transit stage to ensure that everything stays on track and that the carrier does not miss appointments.

Freight brokers also help carriers with directions when they get lost during the transit of the freight. They also act as liaisons between the world and the carriers since they inform drivers about the hurdles they may experience ahead of their journeys like weather delays or traffic.

- *Delivery and unloading:* Once a carrier arrives at the specified destination, the driver is required to document the arrival time in case there are any delays at the drop off site. If a carrier waits beyond a specific time, they end up getting charged for the delays.

Once the carrier offloads the freight, the consignee goes ahead and signs, noting any damages or shortages. Once they sign these documents, they accept possession of the delivered products. The consignee later documents the time the freight arrived and when it was unloaded. The freight broker then waits for the carrier to turn over their paperwork for the shipper to invoice, and the carrier's payments can also be released.

- *Billing:* Once the freight broker receives the carrier's invoice and the necessary paperwork from the shipper, the freight brokers start processing invoices and sending out bills. Some of the vital paperwork freight brokers require to create invoices includes driver work receipts, BOL, rate confirmation, and lumper receipts. These are documents they need to create for the invoice they need to send to the shippers.

Benefits of starting a freight brokerage business

1. Unlimited earning potential

The reason why a majority of people choose a certain career is primarily because of the amount of money they can make from their jobs in a month. One of the best advantages of starting a freight brokerage business compared to other business ventures is that you are paid on commission. This means that there is neither a high or low salary figure that you can earn as a freight broker.

Freight brokerage businesses get compensation based on the amount of money the company makes from either booking a load or moving it. Starting a freight brokerage business is an excellent opportunity for motivated and self-starter individuals to step out of the norm of relying on the 9 am to 5 pm paycheck and start a business with unlimited earning potential.

Since your productivity determines the income of this business, you have the capability of making huge earnings depending on the amount of work you put into your business. Starting a freight brokerage business allows you not to limit your earnings; after all, the top income earners in the freight brokerage business earn six figures every year and some even go higher than that.

2. Flexible scheduling

Another beneficial advantage of starting a freight brokerage business over other businesses is the flexible scheduling this business offers. Having a freight brokerage business means that you no longer get compensation based on the amount of time you spend working, rather you get paid based on how much money your company generates. Since you no longer acquire a payment based on time, you are therefore free to work anywhere and however much you please.

This does not necessarily mean that you have to increase or lower your working hours; it merely means that you get the opportunity to choose what time you want to work and where you want to work. For individuals with families, starting a freight business will give you a chance to work from home making it easy for you to spend more time with your loved ones and earn money while doing so.

You also acquire the opportunity to take time off without having to explain to anyone why you did so. Therefore, if you want a business opportunity that offers you the freedom to fix your schedule to suit your life, why not try the freight brokerage business.

3. Plenty of opportunities

The export and import industry is one of the largest and fastest growing sectors in the world. The reason for this is that almost every country around the globe builds its economy through the exports they make and the imports they acquire from other countries.

The growth of this sector has also led to the growth of the freight industry. In the USA alone, the freight industry has grown tremendously over the years making it possible for other aspects of this industry to improve as well. An increase in growth means that there are plenty of opportunities in the freight industry.

Once you start a freight brokerage business, you do have a

guarantee that there are plenty of opportunities that will help you grow your business and acquire revenue. Unlike other business opportunities, freight brokers can run their business throughout the year without fear of losing their clients or business opportunities despite the season. Learning how to cultivate a long-lasting relationship with your clients as a freight broker helps in ensuring that you have business all year round.

4. No education is required

A freight broker career is one of those careers that disregard the notion that you need a college degree or any other education certificate to succeed in running a freight brokerage business. Do not get me wrong, education is essential, but it does not determine the success of your business as a freight broker.

However, like any other business, starting a freight brokerage business requires you to begin by learning about the industry, as this will enable you to grow your business to greater heights.

Having prior knowledge of the freight industry when starting a freight brokerage business is essential as it helps you learn how to operate your business and speak the freight industry language. It also enables you to form long-lasting relationships with shippers and carriers across the globe because they trust what you do.

It is essential to remember that building a reputable freight brokerage business takes hard work, determination, and patience.

Therefore, if your education level has you worried, no worries; you can choose to incorporate education along the way as you grow your freight brokerage business.

5. *You increase your earnings*

As I mentioned earlier, the freight industry is growing, and this means that the number of merchandise goods and cargo that manufacturers will have to transport to their clients will also increase. This means that anyone who capitalizes on the growth of the freight industry will ultimately reap huge benefits.

One sure way of capitalizing on this industry is through starting a freight brokerage business. This means that you do not have to settle for a specific amount of revenue since your company has the capacity of regularly increasing its profits.

The amount of work and determination you put into your business will also determine how high your earnings are at the end of the year.

6. *Work-life balance*

One of the most common attributes about any career in our modern society is finding a job or starting a business that allows you to balance your professional life and your personal life. A majority of employees who work 9 am to 5 pm jobs only get a two-week leave that are either paid for or unpaid for.

They also get three sick days, a few months for maternity leave, and a few other official leave days that are sometimes not enough to make a difference in someone's personal life.

Starting a freight brokerage business gives you the opportunity to balance your work and personal life without any interference. Unlike having a regular job, you can balance your work life without relying on someone else to do that for you.

You can plan for vacations, take sick days, have kids, or get married whenever you please without asking for permission from anyone.

Since you are not compensated for your time, you have the freedom to balance your work life and still grow your business. You also get to slot in your activities quite easily without it being dependent on your business schedule.

7. You create a legacy

One of the primary objectives of starting a business is building a legacy that will last even after you are no longer alive. You also get to impact your society with the services you offer.

One unique ability every business owner has in their community is the ability to elevate individuals and change their perception towards starting a freight brokerage business.

It gives you the opportunity to value your progress. It also offers complete transparency when it comes to the successes and failures of your business. Each success or failure you experience when growing your business helps influence future decisions.

Your family, clients, employees, and friends will long remember the efforts you put into your business. They will also not forget the influence you had in their lives. You also get to pass down the business you start to your future generation, creating a legacy that your family can inherit.

Starting a freight brokerage business is your opportunity to not only position yourself in the freight industry but it also allows you to put your family and future generations in a place they can continuously succeed.

You also get to create job opportunities, give back to the community, and provide valuable services that will also help support other growing businesses. After all, it's often said that the success of a company is not measured by the amount of revenue it makes, but its impact on society.

8. You do not have a boss to answer to

I am pretty sure not everyone gets along with their bosses, and this can cause your working environment to be quite stressful. Starting a freight brokerage business helps eliminate such an issue. You can work without having someone micromanage your every move. You acquire the freedom to work independently without butting heads with your boss.

Working in a stress-free environment makes you productive, and it also helps clear your mind, making it easy for you to make the right decisions to promote the growth of your business.

9. No territory restrictions

Working as a freight broker is an exciting experience primarily because of the limited limitations it has in the world. Starting this business allows you to offer your services to clients across the country or the globe. Due to the importance of the freight industry to the world's economy, it is possible for freight brokers to grow their businesses without having territorial restrictions.

This offers excellent opportunities to scale up their businesses and brands to provide the best services to their clients. Having no geographical limitations makes it possible for you to build contacts beyond your boundaries. It also offers you the opportunity to grow your business through referrals.

10. Zero commute hours

One wish that a majority of people have when it comes to their careers is to have a job that allows them to work from home and earn an excellent income. Unfortunately, only a few jobs offer such an opportunity. Starting a freight brokerage business gives you the chance to work from home and still make good money.

You no longer have to worry about traveling costs or jam delays. You get to enjoy your sleep, wake up at your own leisure, work in your pajamas, and sleep at whatever time you desire.

11. Minimal monthly overhead

Running a freight brokerage business compared to other companies has minimal monthly overhead costs compared to the running costs of other companies. When you compare the amount of money you require to run a freight brokerage business, other companies rack up more expenses. Hence, starting a freight brokerage business is much better than owning any other company, especially financially speaking.

12. Low start-up costs

A majority of people often think that starting a business requires them to incur plenty of expenses. However, this is not true about starting a freight company. It does not need quite a lot of revenue to start.

All the above advantages prove that a freight brokerage

business is quite lucrative and investing in this business comes with numerous opportunities. Not only can you make a decent amount of money from this business but you also get to influence the community.

You also get to interact with clients from all over the world creating a network that ensures you get long lasting clients and a network that makes it easy for you to get work throughout the year.

However, very few people are willing to start this business due to the misconceptions that surround this industry. Breaking down these misconceptions will help you learn the truth about this industry and disregard the myths.

Misconceptions about the freight brokerage business

Some of the misconceptions a majority of people have about the freight brokerage business include:

Myth 1: Freight businesses are expensive to start

This is one of the most common myths among people who do not have any knowledge on how to start a freight brokerage business. A majority of people tend to shy away from starting a freight brokerage business primarily due to the costs they think they will incur.

However, the fact is the expenses incurred when starting a freight brokerage business are too little compared to that of starting any other business. Some of the expenses when new in the industry are for the purchase of licenses and surety bonds. The license is essential as it helps legalize your business while the surety bond holds you accountable to your clients and prevents you from doing unlawful business practices.

Myth 2: Freight brokers are unreliable

It is often said that one rotten apple does not define the character of the rest of the apples. The fact is in the freight brokerage business, there are a few unreliable freight brokers, but that does not mean that all of them are bad.

For those of you looking to start a freight brokerage business, legislatures have found a way by increasing surety bonds from $10,000 to $75,000 to enhance trust between the customers and the freight broker.

This may seem like an expensive cost to bear while starting a business but it has produced positive results for the freight brokerage industry. If a broker fails to honor the agreement of the client's contract, the affected party can make a claim for compensation for up to $75,000.

Such measures have slowly helped clients gain back the trust and respect they once had for the freight brokerage industry. It also helps keep individuals with the intention of conducting unlawful practices away from the freight industry.

Myth 3: You answer to numerous people once you start your business

Another fear that a majority of people have when it comes to starting a freight brokerage business is that they will be reporting to numerous people. This myth can be quite limiting especially for individuals looking to start their business to be their own bosses.

The fact of the matter is that freight brokerage businesses do not report to numerous people. They directly work hand in hand with other freight companies to ensure the safe delivery of merchandise goods and cargo from the manufacturers to their consumers.

Some of the businesses that freight brokerage companies collaborate with include freight forwarding companies as well as freight transportation companies. Working with these two companies helps coordinate the storage, shipment, and transportation of cargo from one place to another on behalf of their client.

It also makes it easy for the brokerage company to communicate with the shipper and the carrier without having any complications along the way.

Myth 4: All you require to start a freight brokerage business is a freight website

Another common mistake people make is thinking that all they need is a freight business website. Sorry to burst your bubble but the truth is you require more than just a freight website to start a brokerage business.

Don't get me wrong, it is quite essential for any business to develop some income leads through online platforms, but you also need to form a network of carriers and shippers and learn how to communicate with them.

This is where most of your operational costs come about. Having a toll free number and a fax number comes in handy when communicating with shippers and carriers directly. Obtaining these essential services is not as expensive as you may think. All you need for your toll-free number, fax number, and online expenses would be approximately $100 every month. This is such a small expense compared to other costs that other companies incur.

Myth 5: Being a starter company, it is impossible to get carrier contacts from bigger familiar carrier companies

Another common misconception is that it is impossible to get carrier contacts with bigger familiar carrier companies. In the freight brokerage industry, the more freight your business is required to move, the more space you fill on a truck, resulting in you saving more when transporting the cargo.

This means that the more volume you build for the shippers, you also get to develop a good rapport with the carrier. Having an excellent reputation with the carriers guarantees your business a constant flow of transportation for the goods you ship on behalf of your client.

Myth 6: I do not need to know anything about the freight industry to succeed in a freight brokerage business.

A majority of people think that starting a freight business does not require any prior knowledge of the freight industry. Although this may be true to some extent, it's not totally accurate. Knowing this industry makes it easy for you to understand the various processes required for you to perform your duties effectively as a freight broker.

A successful freight broker not only knows the basics of this industry but also learns more than what everyone knows about it. They go the extra mile to ensure they not only learn about their responsibilities alone but those of their carriers and shippers as well.

However, do not let your lack of knowledge about this industry intimidate you, the freight brokerage industry is continually changing, and this gives everyone an equal learning curve.

I hope the information above clears the misconceptions that surround the freight brokerage business. Considering all the requirements and costs other businesses incur, starting a freight brokerage business is not at all that bad. All you have to do is offer your customers quality and value services, and this will help you stay afloat and succeed in your business.

Chapter Two: Necessary Steps to Become a Freight Broker

In this chapter, we will discuss the necessary steps that are needed to be taken to become a successful freight broker. We will also look at the essential knowledge you require to become a freight broker and the importance of attending freight broker boot camps, freight classes, or freight schools.

We will also take an in-depth look at the business entities you require before starting a freight brokerage business.

Here are the necessary steps you need to take to become a successful freight broker.

Step 1: Gain industry experience and knowledge

The first and most crucial step for anyone in becoming a successful freight broker is gaining enough industry experience and knowledge. While a freight brokering business may not require you to have prior experience and knowledge, you can still acquire the knowledge and expertise you need to be the best in this field through diligence and patience. So, how exactly can you gain these things to make it in the freight broker sector?

1. Development or refreshment of some general skills

The first and most important skill any freight broker should possess is a strong will. A strong will is necessary as it helps freight brokers make it through especially when business is not going exactly as you may have planned. Other essential skills you require to develop or refresh as a freight broker include:

- *Strategy skills:* Strategy skills are among the most significant skills needed to make you successful as a freight broker. With the various links along the supply chain required for you to safely transport merchandise goods from one location to another, you need to have the capability to come up with creative strategies that will help you get the job done.

Strategic skills are not inborn, you need to improve them continually or else your freight brokerage business can become dysfunctional. Deliveries may end up not getting to their destinations on time, and this can cause you to lose your business eventually. Once you learn to hone in your strategic skill, you also start succeeding as a freight broker.

- *Organization skills:* Starting a freight brokerage business means that you will be in charge of all the work done within your agency. This entails working independently, and it can be quite a challenge for an individual not used to working without assistance. You become your own booker, personal assistant, scheduler, financial planner, and strategist. On top of all these new responsibilities, you have to ensure you manage the daily influx of orders and requests.

Without organization skills, it becomes relatively impossible to compete with other freight brokers in the industry. Developing your organizational skills will help set your business apart from other freight brokerage agencies in the industry. Strong organizational skills will enable you to offer your clients high-quality services and remain proactive in the industry.

- *Communication skills:* Communication skills are also essential primarily because being a freight broker requires you to communicate regularly with your clients either via email or over the phone. Your communication skills can either make or break your customer relationships. You also require communication skills to negotiate and close deals.

Refreshing your communication skills enables you to stay ahead of your competitors since you can properly relate with your clients and this allows you to offer them quality services.

- *People skills:* People skills in the freight broker industry go beyond treating your employees with respect and helping your clients. It involves your ability to connect with your clients and vendors. If your daily interactions with vendors and clients are fraught with misunderstandings and tension, then there is a big problem with your communication skills.

A freight broker with exceptional people skills has the ability to express him or herself in an understanding and respectful manner especially when under pressure. They also make it their primary goal to help their vendors, clients, and customers get the job done no matter what the obstacles are. People skills do come in handy in helping you maintain your business as it enables you to create long-lasting relationships and networks in the industry.

- *Management skills:* Successful freight brokers are excellent managers of every shipping task they are entrusted with by their clients. Any successful freight broker can tell you that it is quite easy to get overwhelmed by the numerous tasks you are required to perform. This is where you put your management skills to work and lighten the workload.

Management skills help you delegate tasks accordingly, that is in case you have employees. But if you are working on your own, you are able to delegate your tasks in a manner that will not overwhelm you. The ability to exercise your management skills requires you to have excellent knowledge about this industry; you should also know your responsibilities, and learn what interpersonal skills you need to become a successful freight broker.

- *Business skills:* Every successful freight broker requires a business for them to grow, develop, and increase their earnings. You will need to build your business, and this will need some business skills, and they include:

Financial planning: Financial planning helps you plan finances in advance over the long-term, and this keeps your business from failing.

Negotiating prowess: whether you are negotiating with a client or a national carrier or merely trying to figure out the right commission rate you require, negotiation skills help you maximize profits.

Marketing knowledge: Thanks to technology, marketing skills have become a necessary tool for individuals to grow their businesses. Having marketing knowledge is quite essential for freight brokers who want to succeed in their businesses.

- *Networking skills:* Building a list of contacts and clients as a freight broker requires networking skills. As you are building connections, you also have to be strategic with the connections you make. Carefully think about the contacts that can help grow your business both indirectly and directly and then start networking.

Just because you work independently, it does not mean that you do not require other people for you to succeed as a freight broker. In addition, networking with other freight brokerage businesses is also another way for you to unlock the potential your business has by creating smart connections with other businesses.

- *Multi-tasking skills:* Every successful freight broker can tell you that having the ability to handle more than one task is essential in this industry. For instance, the first part of your day could be spent building your clientele while the remaining portion of your day can be spent contacting vendors and processing invoices. At the same time, you could also be in contact with drivers moving the freight.

Balancing all these activities requires you to have multi-tasking skills. However, before you get to the level where you can handle taking on two tasks at once, start small and build up your capacity to tackle more than one responsibility.

- *Technical skills:* Thanks to technology, the freight industry has improved tremendously in the quality of services they offer. This means that your ability to compete in the freight broker industry will be dependent on your technical skills. You therefore have to be ready to integrate technology into your business, making it more efficient and cost-effective for your clients and you.

You also have to start figuring out ways you can integrate driverless carriers into your business along with other beneficial services.

- *Compliance skills:* Every state and city has its own rules for hauling freight. Knowing these regulations may not be part of your job description, but it is essential for you to understand and comply with the rules of different states as a freight broker.

This will help prevent your loads from being stopped during transportation because you did not comply with a particular regulation.

- *Logistics planning skills*: Customers look for freight broker services because they require logistics support when transporting their freight. As the freight broker, your customers are counting on you to act as an intermediary between the shippers and carriers and ensure the safe transportation of their freight. This is where logistics planning skills come in handy.

Logistics planning skills help you offer your clients information about the specific routes they can use to transport their freight. You are also able to analyze the information and provide them advice they can use to make the best decisions.

2. Taking freight brokerage training

Besides having the skills I have listed above, you also require knowledge about the freight broker industry that you can acquire by attending a freight broker school or taking freight broker courses. These courses help you prepare and learn about the actual requirements and responsibilities of your job as a freight broker. Apart from paying for freight broker training courses, you can also look for the best freight broker books for you to constantly refer to when you're unsure of what to do when running your business.

However, the best option to acquire freight broker training is through attending freight broker classes. Thanks to technology, you can now have access to other freight broker courses; which begs the question, how do you choose the right course among numerous courses?

The first step is through conducting a simple online search, and this will yield numerous results. Next, visit the website of the schools that interest you, look at the cost of the training, the length of time for each course, and the school's program offering.

Some of the schools that offer online programs, which train students to become exceptional freight brokers are California State University that has a freight broker certificate program, the University of Houston and the California East Bay State University.

What can you learn from freight broker courses?

Freight broker courses enable freight brokers to develop the skills required to take the Federal Motor Carrier Safety Administration (FMCSA) broker's license exam. Though you may not need this license to practice as a freight broker, you require it to start a freight brokerage business. You will also learn how to start and operate a freight brokerage company.

You will get to learn the history of the freight industry and its unique points. You will also learn the differences between freight brokers, freight agents, and freight forwarders. You also get to learn record-keeping practices that enable you to organize your business appropriately.

You will get to learn how to prepare industry contacts and appropriate documentation for your freight brokerage business, how to contact potential clients and market your business.

Investing in freight broker courses gives you a deep insight into how the industry works as well as the main players of the industry. You also acquire practical knowledge about your responsibilities as a freight broker. Let us not forget that the training you receive from these courses can also open doors of opportunity for your business.

Whatever course you settle for, ensure that it is one that offers sufficient training about the freight industry and an in-depth working of this industry.

Step 2: Choose your company name

Every business requires an identity, and in order to operate a freight brokerage business, the first step is choosing a company name. However, selecting the appropriate name for your business can be an engaging task. Here are some tips that will help make it easy for you to choose the right name for your business.

- <u>Your company name should be unique and unforgettable:</u> The name you choose for your company should stand out from the crowd. It should be catchy, as this will help it remain fresh and memorable in the minds of your clients and potential market.

- <u>Avoid unusual spellings:</u> When coming up with the right name for your company, stay with words your clients can easily spell. A majority of people often choose to select unusual words for their business to make the name of their business unique. This can, however, prove to be a problem when your customers try to search your name or refer your company to someone else. Ensure that you also stay away from a name that will cause you to take time explaining how you came up with the name.

- <u>Keep the name simple:</u> The shorter your company name is, the better. Ensure that you limit the name you choose to two syllables. Avoid special characters and the use of hyphens in the name you select. Since directory listings and specific algorithms work in alphabetical order, ensure that you choose a name that is closer to the letter A than Z. Currently, it would also help if you select a name that can easily turn into a verb.

- <u>It should be easy to pronounce</u>: Forget long phrases and made up words. When coming up with a business name, ensure it is one that your customers can remember and pronounce quite easily. Also, do away with the acronyms, as acronyms do not have much meaning to your clients. When choosing a name for your clients, keep it simple and straightforward.

- The name should make sense: Sometimes business people opt to choose quirky names that do not make much sense. When selecting your business name, try to ensure that the name is not an ambiguous word in a different language.

- Make sure the name you select is available: This may sound like an obvious tip, but if you fail to ensure the availability of the name, it can cost you dearly. The name you choose for your company and its internet domain should be the same. Therefore, ensure that the name you prefer is available by visiting your State Incorporation site, the U.S. Patent Office to check whether the name is already a trademark, and for the domain name check Network Solutions.

- Give a clue: Try to come up with a name that suggests to your customers what you do before you even explain it to them. Ensuring that your business name matches your business makes it easier for your clients to remember the services you offer.

- Sample potential clients: One way of finding out whether the name you select has a positive impact on the image of your business is by sampling it with potential clients. You can do this with different choices and choose the name that gives off an impression with your potential clients.

- Favor common suffixes: Everyone assumes that your company name is your domain name. Therefore, ensure that you favor common suffixes for the name rather than settling for suffixes that are not quite common among your clients.

- Don't allow your company name to box you in: Avoid picking a company name that will not allow your business to include an extra service or move around. This means trying to avoid a company name that has geographical locations or includes product categories. These specifics may end up confusing your clients when you plan to expand your company to a specific geographic area.

The company name you choose will have a direct impact on how your clients view your business. Therefore, think it through before assigning your business any name.

Step 3: Register your business

Once you have a company name, the next step is registering the business. A new business must be registered with the appropriate local government and state agencies to operate.

The type of business determines the requirements government agencies impose. Failure to register your business correctly can result in the closure of your business, hefty fines, and penalties. Here is a step-by-step procedure on how to register your business.

1. Register your business name: Registration of your business name in your local government agency is a sure way of finding out if your business shares the same business name with another company. A majority of states prohibit the use of the same name by two businesses in the same state.

Before you register your company, conduct a name availability search using the secretary of state's website. This will help you identify whether the name you have for your company is in use, in reserve, or held by another business in the state.

Furthermore, companies in any state cannot use names that have already been trademarked by other companies.

2. Decide on the legal structure of your business: Every business is required to choose a legal structure. According to the law, businesses may form as a partnership, sole proprietorship, corporation, LLC, or LPP. The structure you choose for your business will have tax and legal implications for your business.

For instance, sole proprietorship businesses have the ability to figure out their businesses' losses and profits from their individual tax returns. While corporations, LLC, and LLP's need to file the proper documents in the government state agency where their business operates. The filing of these documents takes place in the secretary of state office in the county your company operates from.

3. Request for a federal tax identification number: Once you determine the structure of your business, the next step is to request for a federal tax identification number. You get this information from the Internal Revenue Service. The business website of the internal revenue service states that every LLC, Corporation, partnership, and businesses that have employees need to apply for the federal tax identification number.

Businesses can apply for the tax ID number using the internal revenue service website, by fax, mail, or phone. Applying online or via phone allows the internal revenue service to issue federal tax ID numbers that businesses can use immediately. Businesses that choose to apply for their tax ID number via mail have to wait for approximately four weeks to receive their tax ID numbers. Businesses that opt to use fax have to wait for four business days.

4. Register your company with the department of revenue in your state: Once you obtain a tax ID number, the next step is to register your company with the department of revenue in your state. States differ regarding tax laws, and this is why it is essential for you to register your company in the state where your business resides in.

All states require every business that has employees to register for unemployment taxes and worker's compensation insurance. To register your business with the department of revenue, you need to present your business formation documents.

5. Apply for licenses and permits your business requires in order to operate: This is the final step of registering your company. The permits and licenses your business requires depends on the type of business. Certain businesses like architects, lawyers, and barbers require occupational licenses, which are issued by the state. While other businesses require a general license to operate legally in the country where the business is located. In the case of freight brokerage, one of the licenses required is the Broker Authority license which allows a person or company to act as a freight broker.

Once you go through all the above steps, you can now consider your business legally registered and ready to start operating officially.

Step 4: Develop a business plan

Another important step that is essential for you to become a successful freight broker is developing a business plan. When a business plan is done correctly, it becomes more than a worded document that tells you what to do.

It gives your business a sense of direction and tells you and your employees what the future might have in store for the company. A well thought out plan enables you to map out the future of your freight brokerage business in detail.

It takes into account your goals and resources you have for your business and explains what you require to do for your business to reach great heights and make enormous profits. A business plan can also help you do the following:

Find funding for your business: Every business requires financing for it to start. As a fresh entrepreneur, one of the places you may start looking for funds is through capital investment or from your bank by applying for a line of credit. Your business plan enables your bank to look at how viable your business idea is and opt to either offer you a loan or deny you the finances you require.

Your consultants also write on the business plan, and they give investors reasons as to why they should support your business with the capital you require.

Manage your business growth: Numerous things are going to change once your business starts to grow. First, your yearly budget increases or decreases depending on the expenses of your business. The number of your employees increases and finally your client and financial targets had increased compared to when you first started your business.

As a business owner, it is your responsibility to keep on top of these changes. Your business plan helps you monitor and assess how your business has evolved. It also allows you to note down ways you can continue to grow your business in the future.

Monitor and determine your business objectives: An integral part of success in any business even as a freight broker is your ability to set objectives you can follow through with to ensure your business remains successful. A business plan gives you the opportunity to decide, set, and keep track of your goals. You can tell how your business is doing currently and how far you want it to be in the coming months.

Manage employee and organizational requirements: Having a business plan enables you to figure out who among your employees can fill in a specific role in your business. This enables you to delegate tasks based on the experience of your staff and recruit new employers if need be.

Deliver your market approach: Developing a business plan enables you to determine your target audience. You can plan for clients you require and use your resources to market your business.

A business plan is like an important foundation and implementation roadmap for your business. It shows you how to conduct and start your business.

It also helps you assess your business's present and forecast its future. Having a clear vision of what you want your business to look like increases your chances of success.

Step 5: Find the right carriers

A freight brokerage business that lacks carriers is similar to a ship missing its sails. Part of your marketing mission to become a successful freight broker should be finding the right carriers you can work with that are in the freight industry. So, how do you go about choosing the right carriers as a freight broker?

- Networking: Networking is an essential skill in the freight brokerage business. One of the easiest ways for a freight business to find the right carriers is through referrals. Being relevantly new to the industry should not be an excuse for you when looking for the right carriers. If you do not know any other freight brokers, you can easily network with them by joining industry organizations like the Transportation Intermediaries Association.

The transport intermediaries association is a freight broker community that offers you the chance to build relationships, get educated about important aspects of this industry, and access resources. As a member of such an organization, it becomes a guarantee that fellow freight brokers will assist you with referrals to carrier companies that are reliable and quite professional.

You also receive information on fraudulent operations, unauthorized brokering of shipments, cancellations, theft, and unjustified loss of merchandise goods.

- Attract what you desire: One of the most efficient ways of finding the right carriers for your business is through becoming a reliable and professional freight broker. That implies that you have to treat other people with respect and ethically conduct your business. If you respect your carriers, pay them on time, and communicate professionally with them, then you are most likely to have carriers that are reliable, professional, and trustworthy.

On the other hand, if you do not respect your carriers and you end up treating them disrespectfully, your carriers will end up treating you and your business the same way. Carriers talk, and if you treat them respectfully, you will always have reliable and trustworthy carriers to rely on.

- Get value for your money: If you require a life-saving operation that will help remove a life-threatening tumor, would you go to a back street to find an unlicensed doctor and inquire about their best rates? In such a situation, your best option would be a qualified, experienced, and credentialed doctor. Why would this be? The reason for this is that you are sure a credentialed doctor will remove the tumor and save your life. No matter what the rate is they ask for, you are sure they will deliver. The same case applies to the carriers you work with.

Low- paying loads will definitely attract low-quality services. To get the best carriers, be ready to pay for the right services. Therefore, when looking for the right carriers for your business, try to look for services that are neither too low nor too high.

Do not double-broker carriers: Finally, another way of finding the right carrier for your business is through never double brokering your carriers. It is important to note that there is a significant difference between co-brokering and double brokering.

Double brokering is illegal and this can cause legal battles especially from customers who entrust you with their freight. Double brokering happens when a licensed and legal broker decides to give a load to another broker who is then responsible for finding a carrier.

You may be asking yourself how fraudulent this is. Let me fill you in; fraud comes into play when the subsequent carrier is not legitimate and never intends to pay. The second broker sends its invoice to the first broker and then does a disappearing act after getting paid.

If you deal respectfully with your carriers, then you can be sure that you will find the right carrier for your freight brokerage business.

Step 6: Apply to get a USDOT Number

Once you have gotten acquainted with your roles and responsibilities as a freight broker, what courses you require to take to learn more about the freight brokerage business, and developed a business plan, it is time for you to start the legal procedures you require. Before you start operating in the freight brokerage business, you require a freight broker license, which you can obtain from the Federal Motor Carrier Safety Administration (FMCSA).

This license is also known as the Motor Carrier Operating Authority (MC authority). Before we even get to the steps taken to apply for a USDOT Number, let us first define what a USDOT Number is and what the benefits are of having this number.

A USDOT number is a number that serves as an exceptional identifier for freight companies when monitoring and collecting a company's safety information during crash investigations, audits, compliance reviews, and inspections. This number allows the Federal Motor Carrier Safety Administration to monitor a company during these procedures. Why is the USDOT number so important?

It is the law: If you are in the freight brokerage business, having a USDOT number is very important. What are the requirements for a business to acquire a USDOT number? If your business meets any of the following qualifications, then you require a USDOT number.

- A gross contribution weight or a gross vehicle weight of 10,001 lbs. or more

- If your vehicle is used or designed to carry more than eight passengers including the driver

- If your vehicle is used or designed to carry more than fifteen passengers including the driver of the vehicle regardless of the compensation

- If your vehicle transports hazardous material as found by the Secretary of Transportation.

If your business fits any of the requirements, you do require a USDOT number. Aside from the above requirements, a majority of states still require businesses in the freight industry to have one.

Benefits of a USDOT number

It enables the government to legitimize your business: By acquiring a USDOT number, your business, clients, and carriers know that you are a trustworthy freight broker, who is willing to put in the effort and time to protect their goods and services. You also legitimize your business, making it easy for potential clients to better trust your services without having doubts about whether you will deliver.

For safety purposes: It may not seem like an obvious reason to have a USDOT number but having one ensures the safety of your carriers and employees. This number helps the Federal Motor Carrier Safety Administration (FMCSA) monitor your company's safety record along with other requirements like compliance reviews and crash investigations among others.

This helps to further certify your business as legitimate, reliable, and one that cares about its employees and careers. This number may seem quite restrictive at first, but it eventually becomes part of your business, as its main purpose is to ensure the safety of your business and employees.

How do you obtain a USDOT number? You can obtain a USDOT number through the department of transport website and via phone.

Step 7: Get your broker authority

Once you get your USDOT number, you can then start the registration process to acquire a license from the Federal Motor Carrier Safety Administration (FMCSA). You register by filling in the OP-1 form, which is the freight broker license application form.

You will be required to pay a $300 one-time application fee when registering for a freight broker license. Some of the required information to fill in when applying for the license includes operating authority, insurance, and a process agent among others.

The processing time for the license can take approximately four to six weeks to get approved. Once your license application is approved, the Federal Motor Carrier Safety Administration (FMCSA) sends you the MC number via your email.

However, the issuing of the MC number does not necessarily mean that you can start your freight business immediately. Once the MC number is issued, it gets posted by FMCSA on its registration page.

The FMCSA then gives anyone with a problem concerning your review a chance protest the registration within the next ten days. If no claims are made during this period, then your MC authority is granted.

Step 8: Acquire a Freight Broker bond

Once you obtain the MC number, you require a freight broker bond. It is what will help you acquire your MC authority from the FMCSA.

The purpose of a freight broker bond is to ensure that your business follows all the rules and regulations when conducting business with clients and carriers. In a way, the freight broker bond is an additional line of credit that helps freight brokers take care of cases where contracts were broken or goods were damaged.

The determination of the cost of the freight broker bond depends on three factors, namely your business's credit, your business experience, and the financial strength of your business. Unlike other credit payments, freight broker bond payments allow freight brokers to make payments at a certain percentage annually.

Based on the evaluation of your business strength and credit, your surety is what determines the amount of money you pay every month.

Therefore, the issue of a freight broker bond should not limit you from starting a freight broker business primarily because you do not have to pay the full amount all at once. However, several issues may affect your freight broker bond.

One of these issues includes bad credit. If you have a bad business credit, then your freight broker bond may be relatively higher than what other brokerage businesses pay for theirs.

Bad credit also affects your ability to acquire funding from other sources primarily because you are able to pay. Therefore, ensure when you start a freight brokerage business that you have good credit as this will reduce your freight broker bond and also open opportunities for you to acquire support elsewhere.

Step 9: Obtain cargo insurance

Once your MC number is approved, the next step is to obtain cargo insurance. I am sure we are all familiar with insurance policies, just as your car requires insurance coverage, so does the cargo your clients entrust you to ship for them.

What is cargo insurance?

Cargo insurance offers coverage against damage or physical loss to freight during transportation. The insurance also protects from all external causes of freight damage during the transportation of cargo whether via air, land, or sea. Cargo insurance is also commonly referred to as freight insurance.

It covers transits that are carried out on the road, in the air, on water, by rail, by courier, and registered post parcel. In the International trade of exports and imports, cargo insurance is a necessity. Like any other industry, the freight industry requires cargo insurance as it helps in reducing the risks of exporting and importing goods.

Insurance companies describe cargo to be things such as merchandise, wares, goods, and property among others. The duration of risk attached to the goods starts from when the shipment leaves its place of storage or the warehouse for shippers to begin transporting the cargo.

Benefits of cargo insurance

- It covers you against complete loss of goods at sea

The one thing that every freight broker fears when transporting cargo via sea is the loss of goods at sea. Sometimes accidents happen and some of those accidents cause freight to fall overboard, and this can cause you to get sued for the damages your clients incur.

To prevent your company or the shipping company from taking the blame, you require cargo insurance. According to a survey conducted by the world shipping council, a significant amount of freight is lost every year at sea, and such occurrences result in the complete loss by the owner of the goods and the freight broker. Cargo insurance covers your business and you from such losses.

- Covers your business against accidents that occur at the terminals

Cargo insurance has several policies that ensure your business is protected from losses that may occur at the terminals. Some of the risks could be the destruction of freight by a carrier when moving the cargo from the ship to a truck for transportation. It could also be an accidental drop of the cargo into the sea while loading it for shipping. Whatever the risk may be, cargo insurance ensures that you do not take the losses when such accidents occur.

- It covers your business against accidents that occur when transporting goods locally

As a freight broker, you cannot rule out the possibilities of disasters happening during the transportation of goods locally. Warehouse to warehouse cargo insurance covers you and your business against the losses and risks that occur during the transportation of goods from the exporter's factory to the loading port. It also incorporates losses that happen from the discharge port to the importer's warehouse.

- It covers your business against strike risk and war

One of the factors that affect the import and export business tremendously is war. War can make it quite challenging for freight brokers to ship goods on behalf of their clients primarily because of the risks involved when transporting the goods to war-prone countries. Having a cargo insurance cover policy ensures that you do not have to bear the losses of cargo destruction during the transportation of cargo via ship and on land. This also guarantees your business does not incur the losses experienced during the transportation of freight.

- You require cargo insurance to complete import procedures

One of the requirements in the import and export sector for people that work in the freight industry is that they should have cargo insurance. Some countries demand that businesses in the freight industry should have an insurance certificate when undergoing import operations during the arrival of goods. In such situations, importers end up purchasing cargo insurance before the goods arrive.

In addition, shipping companies also require freight brokers to have cargo insurance coverage before loading their clients' goods on to their ships. This ensures that the shipping company is not liable for any losses or damages the freight may experience during its transportation.

Types of cargo insurance

This type of insurance can be taken for the purpose of domestic and international transportation. However, it does become quite challenging to control and standardize cargo insurance without the appropriate corporation from states and countries primarily because of the different and varying natures of cargo insurance. Considering these differences, cargo insurance is classified as follows.

Marine cargo insurance: Marine cargo insurance provides coverage for cargo transportation by either sea or air. This means that both goods and transportation are covered from the damages that may occur when unloading or loading cargo, piracies, weather contingencies, and other issues that may occur during the transportation of goods. Mostly, marine cargo insurance protects international trade.

Under this insurance, insurance companies offer several policies to their clients. These policies include:

- Specific cargo policies: When any freight business approaches insurance providers or brokers to acquire insurance for a particular consignment, this insurance policy falls under the special cargo policy category. These policies are also referred to as voyage policies mainly because this policy only covers the shipment and not the transportation.

- Open cover cargo policies: When a freight business opts to acquire an insurance coverage against various shipments, you automatically end up activating open cover cargo policies. This type of cargo policy is divided into two categories namely permanent policy and renewable policy. A permanent policy is drawn up for a freight business to be used during a particular period. This cargo insurance policy allows countless shipments during the period the insurance policy is still viable. A renewable policy is issued for a particular value and it requires renewal after its policy expires.

Contingency insurance policy: There are some specific cases where the customer is responsible for insuring the goods against damage or loss and not the seller. One of the losses this insurance coverage protects the seller or the freight broker from is the failure of customers to accept goods when damaged during transportation. In a few cases, customers have been known not to insure their goods and they avoid to take responsibility for the damages of the goods.

In such circumstances, the affected freight brokers end up seeking rectification with the assistance of the legal system. This may end up becoming an expensive alternative, and the outcomes of such a case are either a win or lose type of situation. To avoid this, freight businesses are advised to take contingency insurance policies, which have fewer premium rates.

Land cargo insurance: This type of cargo insurance offers coverage for cargo transportation on land. It covers small utility vehicles and trucks as well. Land cargo insurance covers things like collision damage, theft, and other risks. This insurance policy is domestic in nature, and it usually operates within a nation's boundaries.

Types of coverage offered by cargo insurance

Cargo insurance covers different areas of the freight

industry. It also offers different policies for transportation of goods via air land, or sea. The common types of covers you can acquire from cargo insurance include:

All risk coverage: This policy covers against damage and physical loss of cargo due to external causes. This type of policy covers collision of transportation trucks via an external object, train derailment, deliberate destruction, jettison, deliberate destruction, theft, and adverse weather conditions like lightning or earthquakes, and improper storage.

Shipment-by-shipment coverage: This type of insurance covers the carrier of the person shipping goods on your behalf. However, for this particular coverage, there are some exclusions. Some of these exclusions include criminal acts by the vessel's crew, defects on the transportation vessel, adverse weather conditions, and war.

Free of particular average: the FPA policy is also referred to as the named peril policy. This policy lists what it covers, and it does not cover theft. Some of the things this policy covers include burning, adverse weather conditions, truck overturning, sinking, collision, and stranding.

Step 10: Obtain General liability

Apart from only obtaining cargo insurance, it is also a requirement for freight brokers to obtain general liability. The risks in the freight brokerage business are numerous, and your business requires an insurance policy that protects it from the losses it may incur due to the loss or damage of goods.

General liability is an insurance policy designed to protect freight brokers against freight liabilities due to property damage or bodily injury for the losses that occur. You require both cargo insurance and general liability since most of the shipping companies request that you present them with both before they start working with your business.

Here are some other facts about freight broker insurance you need to know

Ensuring that your freight brokerage business has the right type and amount of insurance is one of the most essential requirements of starting a freight brokerage business. It is, in fact, mandatory for freight businesses to own insurance coverage for them to operate.

Freight broker insurances are quite complex because there are several options to choose from. Understanding the difference between each insurance helps make the appropriate decision in choosing the right insurance coverage for you.

The types of insurance coverage your business requires include:

Broker bond: As I mentioned earlier, every freight broker considering starting a freight brokerage business is required by the federal motor carrier safety administration to carry a broker bond surety amounting to $75,000. This amount is expected to be renewed every year, and it can be paid in installments. The purpose of this bond is to ensure that the freight broker pays the motor carriers and shippers even if the freight broker is unable to fulfill the agreements.

Contingent broker cargo liability: This insurance helps protect your business from damage claims the carrier of the goods will not pay for.

Contingent broker auto liability: This insurance protects your business against any third-party claims like when it is discovered that one of the truck driver's insurance certificate was falsified.

Property insurance and general liability: This insurance covers address liabilities that arise beyond your control involving transport and cargo.

Worker's compensation: Your employees will also require insurance against accidents that happen while on the job. This insurance also covers transportation companies you do business with that do not have worker's compensation.

Different types of insurance require different application procedures

The type of insurance you require as a freight broker varies depending on the freight authority application submitted to the Federal Motor Carrier Safety Administration (FMCSA). For example, if a freight broker submits a BMC-34 form, then they require an insurance policy that covers both damage and loss to property and vehicle.

For freight brokers who submit Form MBC-91X or BMC-91, the insurance policy they seek should cover property damage, bodily injury, and environmental factors.

Ensure that you fill in the insurance forms since the Federal

Motor Carrier Safety Administration (FMCSA) will require them within 90 days from the business's public notice in order for them to fully register your business.

Step 11: Appoint process agents

Once you have already obtained insurance and a surety bond, the next step is to choose or appoint your process agents. The law requires freight brokers to designate a process agent who will operate in every state your business chooses to operate in.

The role of the process agent is to act as a representative for the freight broker upon whom a court of law can serve court papers. Companies have the option of either appointing an individual process agent or an agency that can cover all the states.

Freight brokers appoint process agents through filing a BOC-3 that is provided by the Federal Motor Carrier Safety Administration. Once you fill in the form, you have to submit it to the Federal Motor Carrier Safety Administration for confirmation and approval in order for you to start your business.

Step 12: Get your equipment

Once you have gone through all the above procedures, you need equipment as these are the tools of your trade. A material asset is something every freight broker should consider even if you do not plan to open a physical office during the initial start of your business. So what equipment does a freight broker require?

You'll need technical gears like a computer, fax machine, copier, a printer, a landline, and a mobile phone as well. You should also consider having a strong internet connection as it helps you connect with your carriers and shippers easily online.

You should also consider looking into acquiring a freight brokering software since you can easily automate your work even when working at home and remain productive. As you grow into a successful freight broker, you can start identifying other equipment your services require for you to remain productive and efficient.

Step 13: Get enough starting capital

Unless you already have enough money for you to start putting your freight broker skills to good use in a business, you should then consider securing credit before you even put up your business. Since your business will act as an intermediary between carriers and shippers, you will always be required to pay your carriers even before you receive payment for the shipment of goods. Therefore, ensure that you have enough capital to start your business.

Chapter Summary

- Becoming a successful freight broker does not require you to have an education; but it is, however, essential for you to have knowledge and experience about the freight industry as this is the foundation for you to become a successful freight broker.

- To acquire knowledge and experience about the freight broker industry, you can choose to enroll for a freight broker course or attend freight broker boot camps where you get to learn everything related to this sector.

- All successful freight brokers will tell you that to increase their skills and earnings as freight brokers, they started a freight brokerage business, which gave them hands on experience on how to handle their clients, shippers, and carriers.

- Some of the things freight brokers require in order to be successful in this sector include management skills, people skills, communication skills, multi-tasking skills, negotiation skills, marketing skills, and logistics planning skills among others.

- Some of the other steps involved in becoming a successful freight broker include developing a business plan. This is essential since one of the ways for a freight broker to grow is to start their own business. Another step involves registration of the business, getting a freight broker bond, registering for a USDOT number, obtaining general liability and choosing a process agent. Each of the steps mentioned above has to be taken as they are the starting phase for any individual who wishes to be successful in the freight industry.

Remember, you become successful as a freight broker if you treat your carriers and shippers with respect.

Chapter Three: Setting Up Your Freight Brokerage Business

The next step for any successful broker is setting up a freight brokerage business. In the previous chapter, we highlighted some of the requirements and stages of starting a freight brokerage business.

In this chapter, we are going to look more in depth at the requirements for setting up a freight business. We will discuss each step in detail and look at what is required for you to set up your freight brokerage business. We will also examine some of the things you need to know before you set up your business.

Steps on how to set up your freight brokerage business

Step 1: Come up with a detailed business plan

In the previous chapter, we discussed the importance of a business plan for you to become a successful freight broker. Here, we look at how to come up with a business plan that not only forecasts the future of your business but also one that will give you the funding you require for your business from investors.

How to develop a business plan

Just like in any business, developing a business plan comes with rules and critical elements.

Three golden rules of writing a plan are:

1. Keep the business plan short

Business plans should be concise and brief. The reason for this is that you want people to read your business plan. The longer the business plan, the more tedious it becomes for anyone to read. Honestly, no one is going to read a business plan that is 100 pages long, let alone 40 pages. Secondly, a business plan is a tool you use to grow and run your business. You do not just write it and forget about the plan; you continuously use it and refine it over time. A long business plan becomes a huge hassle for you to deal with and you might end up throwing it in a desk drawer and never use it again.

2. Know your audience

The second golden rule of business plan writing is creating a plan your audience will understand. For instance, since you want to start a freight brokerage business, you need to expand your search for investors to people who do not know the ins and outs of the freight broker industry. Therefore, when coming up with a business plan, ensure that the language you use does not refer a lot to the freight broker sector since your investors may not understand what you mean.

3. Do not be intimidated

A majority of business owners are not financial experts, and it can be quite intimidating to write a business plan if you have never done so before. If you are passionate about the freight brokerage business, then you are mostly ready to set up that business plan and later use it to grow your business. It should not be an uphill task.

In fact, you do not have to start with a detailed business plan; you can start by creating a simple business plan and then continue to build on it as time continues.

The elements of writing a business plan

Before writing your business plan, it is essential to remember that your business plan is a requirement for any freight broker who wants to build their business. It is a living document that you refer to from time to time. You use it to track the course of your business and adjust your business according to the plan you have for your business. Therefore, your business plan should contain

1. An executive summary

An executive summary introduces your business, explains what your company does, and lays out what you as the business owner is looking for to the reader. Structurally, the executive summary is the first chapter of a business plan. It is the first thing your audience gets to read before diving into the rest of the plan. It is often advised that the executive summary be the last thing to write since it is a summary of the other chapters in a business plan.

So starting with the other parts of the business plan and coming back to the executive summary makes it possible for you to highlight everything in the plan. Ensure that your executive summary is clear and concise. Cover all the key highlights of your business and make sure you do not go into much detail. Here are some of the critical elements of an executive summary:

- Business overview: At the top of the page, right beneath your company name, include an overview of your business in one sentence. This sentence is supposed to sum up everything about what you do in your company. Indicating what your business does is quite important, as it is the first thing your audience should see.

- Problem: Summarize the problem your business is solving in one or two sentences. Every freight brokerage business is addressing a particular problem in the freight industry. Clearly, state that problem your company is solving for customers and how your business is filling that need.

- Solution: This section is for the service you are providing in the freight industry. How is your business addressing the problem identified in the freight industry? What skills or expertise are you bringing to the industry to ensure the problem is completely solved?

- Target market: Once you have identified the problem and solution, the next step is identifying your target market. Who is your business targeting? How many people do you want to target? When stating your target market, it is essential for you to be quite specific. For instance, starting a freight brokerage business means that you will not be targeting everyone.

Your particular interest is people in the import and export sector. However, you have to be specific on who precisely you are targeting with your freight brokerage business. Identifying your target market makes your sales and marketing efforts more manageable, and you attract customers that are ready to work with you.

- Competition: Every business including the freight business you are interested in starting has competition, and understanding how your competition is solving problems in the freight industry is important. That is why you have to include your competition strategies when writing a business plan.

- Team: When talking about your team in the executive summary, you have to provide an overview since you will discuss your team later in the business plan. Use a short explanation to explain why you and your team are a perfect fit. Note, a start-up freight business does not require you to have a team, but investors are quite keen on seeing how you and your team will work together. Investors emphasize a lot about the importance of a team when starting a company.

- Financial plan: Highlight the significant aspects of your business financial plan. You can do this with an expenses list, your profitability, or a planned sales plan. If your financial plan requires further explanation, this is where you include the business model you have on how to create the amount of money you need to run your business.

- Funding requirements: If you require money to start your freight brokerage business or grow it, this is where you include the details of your funding requirements. It is important to note that terms like potential investment are not included in this section of the business plan because it can be discussed later. Simply include a sentence that indicates the amount of money you require to raise to start your business.

- Traction and milestone: The last essential part of your executive summary that your investors would want to see is the progress your business has made and the milestones you want to achieve in the future.

In case you are writing an internal business plan, you can opt to skip the executive summary since the business plan you are writing is purely to formulate a strategic guide for your business. You can also choose to forgo details such as funding requirements, traction, and information about your team, and treat the executive summary like a strategic overview of your business, as this will help your management team remain on the same page.

2. An opportunity

The opportunity section is where all the necessary information of a business plan is found. In short, it is the meat of your business plan. In this section, you describe in complete detail what problems your business is going to solve. You also describe who your target customer is and how your service or product fits into the competitive landscape. You will also use the opportunity section to demonstrate how your solutions are different from others in the industry, as well as plan how to expand your business in the future.

The readers of your business plan should learn a little more about your business as this is the section you use to expand your business overview. You also provide further details and answer questions your executive summary does not cover.

- The solution and problem

You start the opportunity chapter of your business plan by describing the problem your business solves for your customers. What is their main pain point? How are your clients solving their problems? Is the existing solution too expensive for your clients? Is the available solution cumbersome? You also have to explain whether the physical location of your business has an existing solution to the problem within a reasonable distance.

Once you have asked yourself the above questions about your business, start by defining the problem your company is solving for your target market. This is the most crucial factor in your business. Identifying the problem also helps your business grow tremendously. If you cannot pinpoint the problem your freight business is solving for your potential customers, then your business concept may not be that viable.

To make sure that your business is solving a real problem for its potential customers, a critical step in the business planning process is to take time away from your computer, approach your potential customers, and talk with them. Once you validate that they do have a problem, you can go ahead and pitch your solution to them and find out if your business solution is viable.

Once you pinpoint the problem your business wants to solve for your potential customers, the next step of writing your business plan is describing the solution to the problem. Your solution is the service or product your freight brokerage business will offer to its potential customers. Ensure you write your solution in detail by asking yourself the following questions. What is your solution? How will you offer your solution? How exactly does the solution your business is offering solve your customers' problems?

You can also choose to include cases of services your freight business will offer to clients as this will show how your service interacts with a customer's life and makes it better.

- Target Market

Once you identify and detail the problem and solution in your business plan, the next step under the opportunity chapter is identifying your target market. Whom are you selling your services to? What you write in this section depends on the type of business you want to start and the business plan you are writing. However, ensure that you identify your target market and estimate how many potential clients there are before you start your freight business. If your potential clients are not enough, that is a huge warning sign.

To help you determine the number of potential clients in your target market, you can use a formal market analysis. This will help you conduct research by first identifying a market segment and later recognizing how large each market segment is. A market segment is the number of businesses or people you could potentially help with your service. While determining your target market, make sure that you do not fall into the common notion of describing your target market as everyone.

- SAM, TAM, and SOM

A good plan will identify its business target market and later provide its readers with data that will indicate how fast a specific market segment is growing. When recognizing your business's target market, you can use the classic SAM, TAM, and SOM method. This helps in breaking down your target market size from a bottom-up approach as well as a top-bottom approach.

The definitions of the above abbreviations are as follows:

- SAM: Served Available Market or Segmented Addressable Market

- TAM: Addressable Market or Total Available Market

- SOM: Share of the market

Once you have identified your target market, you can then proceed to discuss the trends of the freight broker industry. You should recognize whether freight broker market trends are shrinking or growing. You should be able to identify how the needs of the market are evolving, how its tastes are changing, and how other upcoming changes are affecting the market.

The next step is defining your business's ideal customer for every market segment. Your typical customer is a clear representation of your market, and it is also referred to as a user persona or a buyer persona. You should define your buyer persona with a gender, name, likes, income level, and dislikes, among other things.

While this may seem like quite a lot of work to do while writing a business plan, it helps you define your sales and marketing activities that you can use to attract your ideal customers.

- Key customers

The final section of the target market chapter discusses your key customers. This section of your business plan is only a requirement for freight businesses that have a few companies. However, if your business is already making sells to a majority of consumers, then you do not require this section. If your business is new to the industry, then you need to include this section.

If you are offering your services to other businesses, then you do have several key customers who are critical in the success of your business. If this is true for your business, you can use this section to describe your key customers as well as show how essential they are to the success of your business.

- Competition

Once you conclude describing your target market, you should also have a section for competition description. Which other business is trying to solve your customers' pain points? What strong advantages do you have over your business rivals? To define this, plenty of businesses utilize a competitor matrix. A competitor matrix lists your competitors, and you later use that list to compare your competitor's solution against yours.

The most essential thing about creating this list is to ensure that you show how your solution is better than those other freight companies that are offering solutions to your potential customers. If you plan on presenting your business plan to investors, ensure that you clearly state the advantages of your business over your competition and the ways you plan to differentiate your business from other freight brokerage businesses.

One of the mistakes start-up businesses make when coming up with a business plan is stating that they have no competition, which is not true. Every business has competition and identifying this fact will help you stay at the top of your game and offer viable solutions to your potential clients.

- Future services and products

Every businessperson has a specific vision about the future of his or her business. While it may be tempting to expound on your future business ideas and new services, it is best not to go into details when writing a business plan. You can choose to include a paragraph or two about your future services and products.

This section will also show your investors that you are thinking about your business from a long-term perspective, but you do not want your future to derail your present plan for starting and growing your business.

3. An execution

Once you have described the opportunity, the next thing you have to do is explain how you are going to make your freight brokerage business work. In this business plan chapter, you will cover sales and marketing plans, your operations, how you will measure the success of your business, and the milestones you want to achieve.

- Sales and marketing plans

The sales and marketing plans section details how exactly you plan to attract your target market. It also describes how you plan to sell your services to them. It explains your pricing and the type of partnerships and activities your business will require to make it successful. Before you even commence on writing your marketing plan, ensure that you accurately define your target market. You should also have fleshed-out your buyer persona as this makes it easy to understand the customers you are marketing your services to.

- Positioning

The first section of your marketing plan should cover the positioning of your business and the products you are offering. A positioning means how you will present your business to potential customers. You can ask yourself questions like are you going to provide your customers with a lower price for the services you offer? Are you offering the same services as your competitors? You should also consider answering the following questions before you start working on this section.

- What benefits or features are you offering consumers that are different from your competitors?

- What are the primary wants and needs of your customers?

- How do other competitor businesses position themselves?

- Why should your potential consumers choose your services and not those of your competitors?

- Where do you see your business in the development of other solutions?

Once the above questions are answered, you can now start working on your business positioning strategy. Make sure that you clearly define this strategy in your business plan.

- Pricing

Once you state your positioning strategy, the next step is

moving to price. Your positioning strategy is what will determine how you price your services as a freight broker. Your pricing will send a strong message to potential customers that will cause them to either select your services over others or shun you. For instance, you can opt to separate your pricing based on standard, medium, and premium services. Each of these services should have prices that clearly indicate the quality of service your clients should expect to recieve.

Coming up with the prices of your products should not be based solely on feelings; it involves following some basic rules like:

Covering costs: When determining your costs, ensure that you are charging enough to help cover what it costs you to deliver your services or products.

Matching your market rate: The prices of your services should match those of your consumer expectation and demand. If your prices are too high, then you might not get any customers. If your rates are too low, then your customers may end up undervaluing your services.

Primary and secondary profits: Your initial price must not be centered on your primary profits.

Tips to help you strategize your pricing

Cost-plus pricing: You can determine the prices of your services based on a few factors. Simply look at the costs of your services in the market and then mark up your pricing from that point. This strategy is useful for manufacturers whenever they are covering their initial costs.

Value pricing: Another strategy you can use is value pricing. This is where you determine your prices based on a value pricing model. You determine the prices of your services based on the amount of value your services offer to your customer.

Market-based pricing: Another strategy is to use your competitors' current landscape. You can use your competitors' current landscape to create a price based on what your target market expects.

- Promotion

Once you take care of the pricing of your services and the positioning of your business, it is time to think about your promotional strategy. Your business promotional plan should detail your plans as to how you will communicate with customers and prospects. Remember, that as you think about your promotional strategy, you have to measure your promotional costs and the sales they deliver. These programs are not profitable and are hard to maintain for a long period of time.

Here are some of the areas you should consider when thinking about promotion:

Packaging: The packaging of your products and services is quite important. If you have an idea as to how you are going to package your products in your services, be sure to include that in the business plan. Ensure that the packaging idea you come up with is able to answer the following questions.

- Does your packaging idea fit into your positioning strategy?

- How does the packaging of your services as a freight broker communicate your key proposition?

- How does your service package compare to that of your competitors?

Advertising: Your business plan must have an overview of the kind of advertising you will spend to target your customers. Ensure you state whether you will be using traditional media or online platforms to advertise your business. A key component to include in your advertising plan is the measure of success for your advertising.

Content marketing: Another popular strategy you can use to promote your business is content marketing. Content marketing is where you publish useful tips, information, and advice and make it available for free to your intended market. This strategy makes it possible for your target market to learn more about your company from the services you deliver to your expertise in the freight industry.

Content marketing is about educating and teaching your prospective customers on topics; they may be interested in your industry and not just about the benefits and features your company offers.

Social media: Thanks to technology, it has now become a possibility for companies to market their services on social media platforms without having to rely on traditional marketing methods. Remember, you are not required to join all social media platforms to advertise your business, you simply need to join the ones where you can find your customers quite easily.

More and more people are joining social media platforms to learn more about companies and their products. Ensure you use social media to reach customers and enable them to learn more about your company.

- Strategic alliances

Once you complete your marketing plan, the next step is coming up with a strategic partnership that will help your business grow. You can do this by relying on another freight business, not necessarily a broker business, and form a partnership. For instance, you can opt to form an alliance with a transportation company.

This partnership offers you access to a segment of your target market since your partner gets to bring in new clients by providing a new service or product that was not part of their company before. If you already have partnerships established, ensure that you detail them when writing your business plan.

- Operations

After you complete your marketing plan and strategic alliances, the next step is to come up with the operations section. This section details how your business operates. It is the technology and logistics among other items that you need to include. However, the inclusion of this section depends on the type of business you have; you may choose to include or eliminate the sections your company does not offer.

Sourcing and fulfillment: This section is for businesses that buy the products they sell from vendors. In this section, it is essential for you to include details about the source of your product, how these products are delivered to you, and how you ultimately deliver your products to consumers.

For a freight brokerage business, ensure that you detail the operations of your business. It is essential to write how you deliver freight to your clients. You need to know the connections between your business, the carriers, and shippers. This gives a clear picture of how you want your business to operate.

- Distribution

Once you detail your business operations, the next section is your distribution plan. This section completes your business plan. However, since the freight business offers services, simply skip this part when writing your business plan.

- Milestones and metrics

A business plan is merely a written document without an execution plan. It is simply a complete document that details your schedule, responsibilities, and defines roles. The milestones and metrics chapter in a business plan is essential as it helps you look forward and plan for the next steps and direction you want your business to grow.

If you are looking for investors, ensure that you include this section, as they will want to know what happens after you make your business plans a reality. First, start with a review of your milestones. Milestones are simply major goals you want to accomplish as you grow your business. Since you are creating a freight brokerage business plan, ensure that the milestones you talk about in your business plan are related to the freight broker industry.

- Tractions

While milestones highlight your future goals, tractions look at your accomplishments in the past and present. Investors look at this when you present them with your business plan. Tractions are a clear indication of success in the early stages of your business. This could be in the form of a successful pilot, a significant partnership, or initial sales. Sharing the success your business has had in its initial stages affirms that your business is a success and this can cause you to land the finances you require to grow or start the business.

- Metrics

In addition to tractions and milestones, ensure that your business plan contains a detailed explanation of the key metrics you will be watching to help get your business off the ground. Metrics are numbers you use to judge the health and growth of your business. These numbers are drivers of growth for your financial plan and business model. Every business including a freight brokerage business has key metrics it should monitor and watch.

These numbers will help you identify whether your business is in trouble and spot its growth. Ensure you detail the metrics you will be using to track the growth progress of your business.

- Key risks and assumptions

The last section of the execution section in your business plan is the key risks and assumptions section. This is an essential section of your business plan as it is important in the success of your business. Knowing and detailing your risks and assumptions as you start your freight brokerage business makes the difference between business failure and business success. Once you recognize your business assumptions, you are able to prove whether your assumptions are correct. The more assumptions you minimize, the higher the likelihood of your business succeeding.

4. A company and team

The fourth chapter of your business plan is the company and team chapter. In this chapter, you review your company's structure and its key team members. Investors emphasize a lot about such details because they want to learn the team behind your business. They also want to discover whether your team can convert your business idea into a success.

- Team

I am sure you have heard this famous saying, "Investors do not invest in ideas but in people." Some investors even go a notch higher and say that they would invest in an average idea with an excellent team than invest in a great business idea that has an average team. What they mean in that statement is that having a successful business boils down to how you execute your idea. With the right team, you can turn your business idea into a successful business venture in a very short period of time.

The team chapter of your business plan should detail your management team. This is the part of your business plan where you make the best case to investors that you indeed do have an excellent team that can execute your business idea. For a freight business, you can choose to highlight your shippers and carriers since you cannot work without them.

Therefore when writing this brief, ensure that you include brief bios of each team member. It could be a company or individuals. However, if you do not have a management team as of yet, you can still leave this part of the business plan blank until you have one. Finally, you can also choose to include an organizational chart for your business. At some point as your business continues growing, you may be required to have an organizational chart when requesting additional funding.

Apart from raising funds, an organizational chart also helps in planning for the growth of your business over time. It also helps you fill in the roles and responsibilities of the team you have or will include once you get your business off the ground.

- Company overview

A company overview is the shortest section you have when writing a business plan. In case your business plan is simply for sharing with your business partners and team members, then you can omit this section and move on to the next one that follows. But if you plan to show investors your business plan, then you need to detail your company overview.

For a business plan to be shared with people outside your business, ensure you include the following in this section:

Your mission statement: A point to note when creating your mission statement is that it should not take days to come up with. The reason for this is that you will end up with a long, general statement. A mission statement is short and written in one or two sentences. It should encompass everything your business does in those two sentences. It should also encompass your services, as it will build to the kind of marketing you plan to do.

A brief review of your businesses ownership and legal structure: One of the requirements of starting a freight business is that you should decide the legal structure of your business. Ensure that you provide a detailed review of the ownership of your business, as well as the legal structure of your business.

The location of your business: Your company overview should state the location as well as any property the company owns. For businesses that offer services to their clients, this is important especially for freight businesses.

Intellectual property: This section mostly applies to scientific and technological ventures. So you can skip this section because the business you want to start is not scientific or technological.

A brief history of your company: If you're writing a business plan for a company that already exists, mentioning its history is appropriate. If you are just starting your freight business, then skip this section.

- A financial plan

Finally yet importantly is the financial plan section. This is the section that a large majority of entrepreneurs find intimidating to write. It does not have to be that difficult to write. Since you are starting your freight brokerage business, you do not have to worry that much about your financial plan since developing it is not that difficult. A standard financial plan includes monthly financial projections of the first 12 months from when you start your business. Here are some of the things you should include in your financial plan as well as an overview.

Sales forecast: Your sales forecast is simply the projection of the number of sales you are going to make over the next few years. To create a sales forecast, you simply break down this section into rows. Each row should contain the main services you are offering as a freight broker. Breaking down your information into a row system ensures that you do not complicate your sales forecast by explaining things in detail.

You should also include corresponding rows of expenses and cost of goods sold. When it comes to expenses, ensure you include items like insurance, surety bonds, and rent among others.

Personal plan: If you plan to have employees as you start your freight brokerage business, you have to detail how you will pay them. Since your business is small, you can list your whole team and simply state how much each will get per month. Your personal plan should also include an employee burden.

An employee burden is the cost of your employees beyond their salaries. This includes insurance covers, payroll taxes, and other necessary costs you will end up incurring for having employees on your payroll.

Profit and loss statement: Your profit and loss statement is also referred to as your income statement. This is the section of your financial plan that shows whether your business is profiting or making losses. The profit and loss statement gathers data from your personal plan and sales forecast along with other expenses with which you use to run your business.

For businesses that are just starting, you can skip this section and come back to it once your business is off the ground. This statement contains all the necessary information concerning the growth of your business. You can determine whether your business is making a loss or profit as it grows.

A typical profit and loss statement spreadsheet contains the following:

Your sales: The number for the sales your business makes will come from the sales forecast worksheet. It will also include all the cash your business generates.

Cost of goods sold: The number of cost of goods sold will come from the total cost of trading your services and your sales forecast worksheet.

The above statements are just a few of the things you need to include when creating a profit and loss statement.

- Cash flow statement

A majority of businesspeople often presume that a cash flow statement is quite similar to a profit and loss statement. However, each of these statements serves a different purpose from the other. While a profit and loss statement calculates your business losses and profits; a cash flow statement helps you keep track of the amount of money you have in your bank. Having a cash flow statement is important as it informs you when you are running low on cash. You are also able to determine the appropriate time to buy equipment. With a cash flow statement, you can also figure out the amount of money you need to borrow or raise to grow your business. You can use your cash flow statements to figure out when your business is low with cash and this will help keep you from closing the doors.

- Balance sheet

The last essential part of your financial statement to include in your business plan is a balance sheet. A balance sheet will offer you a general overview of the health of your business. It will also list the liabilities, assets, and equity of your business. If you subtract your business liabilities from its assets, you are able to determine the net worth of your business.

- Use of funds

If you are planning to raise funds to start your freight brokerage business, you can include the use of funds section that will detail how you intend to use the money investors offer. You do not have to provide excruciating details about how you intend to use the money; simply provide an overview and show your investors the areas they are most likely interested in. Some of these areas are marketing strategy, sales, and purchasing inventory.

- Exit strategy

The last thing you need to include in your financial plan is an exit strategy for your business. An exit strategy is a plan you have that involves you selling your business to another company or selling it to the public in an IPO. Investors are often keen to listen to business owners when it comes to their business exit strategy. After all, investors also get a share of the returns of your business once you invest. Again, do not detail too much, simply identify companies that would want to buy into your business. Having an exit strategy is also a way of forecasting the future of your business; therefore, ensure you include it.

5. An appendix

The appendix section is not a chapter in a business plan, but it is quite necessary to have one. This section includes useful items that your business plan requires like legal notes, charts, definitions, tables, and other important information that is either out of place or too long to include elsewhere while writing a business plan.

I hope all the information detailed above will help you come up with a business plan that is not only detailed but one that also enables you to acquire the funding you require.

Step 2: Choose the appropriate legal structure for your freight business

Once you create a business plan, the next step is to choose a legal structure for your freight brokerage business. According to law, you have to decide whether you want your business to be a partnership, a sole proprietorship, a limited liability corporation among other options. We will look at the pros and cons of each legal structure since you need to know them before you make any decision. Remember, the legal structure you choose for your business is very important as it determines plenty of things in the business sector.

1. Sole proprietorship

A sole proprietorship business in simple terms is a one-man owned business. This type of business structure is managed and owned by a single individual.

The person who owns and runs a business single-handedly is known as a sole proprietor. The man and the business are the same since sole proprietorship does not have separate legal entities.

Usually, a sole proprietorship business does not require registration or incorporation. It is the simplest form of business an individual can run and an ideal business structure for people with small and medium businesses.

Features of a sole proprietorship business:

- Liability: Since it is impossible to separate the business and the owner, the liability of the owner over his/her business is unlimited. Therefore, if the business were to incur constant losses, the owner has to pay for the expenses the business incurs from his or her own pocket. This can cause the business owner to sell their personal items like a car or a house to meet the liabilities the business incurs.

- It lacks legal formalities: Sole proprietorship businesses often do not have separate laws that govern them. So, there are no special regulations or rules such businesses follow. In most cases for your business to operate, all you require is a license from relevant authorities. And just like the formation of a sole proprietorship, there is no legal structure for the closure of such a business.

Overall, this business structure allows for easy business dealings with minimal hassles when it comes to the legal formalities.

- Risk and profit: The owner of a sole proprietorship business is the sole bearer of the risks the company incurs. Since he/she is the only financial investor of the business, he/she ends up bearing all the risks of the business. If the business suffers a loss or fails the owner of the sole proprietorship business is the only one affected.

However, if the business does well and it increases its profits, he/she gets to enjoy all the additional profits from his/her business. The business owner does not have to share his/her business profits with anyone. Therefore, he/she bears all the risks of business in order for him/her to enjoy the profits of his/her business.

- No separate identity: Another feature that sole proprietorship businesses have is that it becomes quite difficult to separate the owner and the business. In this type of company structure, the owner and business have the same identity. This means that there is no legal identity that can be bestowed upon a sole proprietorship business. So the owner of the business is responsible for all the transactions and activities of the business.

- Continuity: Since the owner and business own the same identity, the sole proprietorship business is totally dependent on its owner for success. The retirement, death, bankruptcy, imprisonment, or the insanity of the owner can affect the business tremendously. In such cases, when the owner no longer runs the business, it ends up closing down.

How is a sole proprietorship business formed?

There is no legal procedure as to how a sole proprietorship business is formed. The business is simply established when a businessperson starts operating their business. This type of business has no separate license, unlike other business structures. A sole proprietorship business will also last as long as the owner keeps the business going.

Benefits of sole proprietorship businesses

One of the most significant advantages of a sole proprietorship business over other business structures is that it is easier to set up. An individual acquires the name 'sole proprietor' by simply opening and running a business.

Another functional advantage of having a sole proprietorship business is that you maintain 100% ownership and control over the business. As a sole proprietor, this helps in facilitating quick decisions and the freedom to conduct business according to your preference.

Sole proprietorship businesses have a significant advantage over other companies when it comes to taxes. In some states, the law does not require sole proprietorship businesses to provide separate tax filings. Instead, what sole proprietorship businesses are required to do is to report their business net loss and net profit when filing personal income tax. This ensures that the sole proprietor does not incur double taxation like other business entities.

Double taxation means that business entities like corporations are taxed twice. The first time is when the corporation makes a profit and the second time is when that profit is paid out to the corporate owners. Sole proprietorship businesses do not undergo such procedures because their business profits are already filed in the owner's personal tax form.

Also, the law does not require sole proprietorship businesses to publish their financial accounts or any business documents to the public. This gives the business a great deal of confidentiality and this is quite important for any business in the world.

The sole proprietor can maximize incentives since he/she does not need to share business profits with anyone else. Therefore, the work the owner puts into his/her business is reciprocated in the form of incentives.

Sole proprietors have no bosses and this gives them a sense of achievement and satisfaction knowing that they are answerable and accountable only to themselves. It also helps in boosting self-worth and confidence knowing that you can make your business succeed despite the obstacles.

Disadvantages

One of the greatest limitations of a sole proprietorship business is that the owner is responsible for unlimited liability. The owner is liable for every loss the business incurs. If the business were to fail, the owner can lose their personal assets when trying to pay off the debts the business may have gathered. This can affect the owner's future as well as negatively impact the owner's health and his/her family's well-being.

Another problem sole proprietorship businesses experience is limited capital for their businesses. Since it is difficult for a sole proprietor business to separate from the owner, the owner bears all the costs of running his/her business.

They end up using savings or borrowing funds to ensure that their businesses run even when they constantly produce losses. Sometimes, banks and financial institutions are quite wary and they tend not to loan finances to sole proprietorship businesses.

The cycle of life for a sole proprietorship business is undecided. The reason for this is that the business is attached to the owner.

If the sole proprietor is incapacitated in any way, the business is affected negatively. This can even cause the business to close. This can be quite a problem because the sole proprietor is the only one who knows the ins and outs of the business.

Unlike other business entities, sole proprietorship businesses have limited managerial abilities. The truth is that no one is an expert in all things.

Limited resources of a sole proprietorship business result in the owner performing all the tasks since they are not able to hire people that are competent in the areas they lack expertise. This causes the business to suffer from poor decisions and mismanagement.

Therefore, if you choose to select a sole proprietorship business structure make sure that you realize you will be responsible for your business. You will also take care of the funding of your business and this can be quite tricky especially if you have limited capital to start.

On the plus side, having a sole proprietorship business means that taxes are different from other business entities. All you need to do is fill in your net losses and net profits in your personal tax form and this exempts you and your business from double taxing, unlike other business entities.

2. Partnership

A partnership legal structure business is one where two or more individuals get together to create a lawful business. They agree to share the losses and profits the business makes during its daily operations.

The management of the business is done by all the partners or by one partner acting on behalf of the other partners. The term partnership arises from the fact that individuals have decided to pull together their resources, money, and skill to come up with a viable and lawful business.

The amount of profits and losses they share is agreed upon using a certain ratio. A majority of partnership businesses often choose to determine this ratio on the number of resources, money, and skills they put into the business.

Characteristics of a partnership:

- Membership: A partnership requires at least two individuals and not more than 100 individuals to start a partnership. Furthermore, the individuals entering into this form of business structure should be legally competent because of the contract they have to sign with their partners.

- Unlimited liability: The members of this type of business structure have an unlimited liability because they are individually and collectively liable for the company's obligations and debts. In the event that business assets are not sufficient to pay off the debts the business has, all the partners have a personal responsibility of repaying the company's liability with their personal assets.

- Voluntary registration: The registration of individuals as a partnership is not compulsory, but the law recommends it due to the numerous benefits partners receive. In the event that there is a conflict between the partners, partners are allowed to file suits against each other or other parties outside of their business.

- Continuity: A partnership form of business has no continuity since the death, bankruptcy, insanity, or retirement of a partner can lead to the end of the partnership. Although, if not all partners experience the above problems, they can create a fresh agreement to ensure their business does not close down.

- Sharing of losses and profits: The primary reason why a majority of people prefer partnership businesses is that they can share profits using an agreed ratio. However, the absence of such an agreement can lead to disagreements between partners.

- Mutual agency: The partnership business is usually undertaken by an agency that represents the interests of the partners. Therefore, every partner is responsible for the running of the business.

- Contractual relationship: The relationship between partners in business is contractual, and it can be in the form of a written agreement, an implied contract, or an oral contract.

Advantages of a partnership

- Two heads or even more managing a business are better than one.

- It is easy to establish the business, and the start-up costs are lower than that of a sole proprietorship business.

- You have more capital available for your business.

- Your business has a larger borrowing capacity unlike other businesses.

- It becomes easy to change the legal structure of your business.

Disadvantages of a partnership

- The liability the partners experience for the debts the business incurs are unlimited. This means every partner has a responsibility to ensure they clear that debt.

- Each partner is joint to the other and is responsible for the debts the business or a partner has when it comes to the company.

- Each partner is responsible for the actions of the other partner.

- If one partner opts to leave, the rest of the partners have to cover the costs of that partner.

3. *Limited liability Company*

A limited liability company is a business entity that is quite popular among small business owners and entrepreneurs. The reason for its popularity is because of its flexibility and liability protection when it comes to operations and tax treatment. While the laws that govern limited liability companies differ from one state to another, some common characteristics govern limited liability companies in all of the states.

Characteristics of a limited liability company

Separate legal existence: One of the most significant characteristics of the limited liability company business structure is that it has a separate legal existence apart from the legal existence of its members. While a group of individuals can run a business together in a contracted partnership, according to the law they are still individuals who incur debt and are one property together.

However, the case is different for limited liability companies. This type of business is a separate legal entity that can sell and buy property, institute lawsuits, hire employees, and retain attorneys who are able to defend their claim as a business.

Limited liability: Just as the name suggests, limited liability companies offer their members limited liability. Although employees, managers, and members are responsible for their civil wrongs, or mistakes, the limited liability company has a responsibility of protecting it managers, members, and employees from liability. This characteristic allows members to hire employees and carry out a high-liability business that would lead to lawsuits in other business structures.

Simplicity in operation and documentation: Despite having a separate legal existence, a limited liability company is characterized by the simplicity of its operations and documentation. Most states do not require limited liability companies to file minutes for annual shareholder meetings they hold. Unlike a corporation, record keeping for a limited liability company is not as tedious.

Flexibility in taxation: Another significant characteristic of a limited liability company is its taxation flexibility. Taxation companies do not have a separate tax category for the LLC, so these businesses end up being taxed as partnership companies or sole proprietorship businesses.

Advantages of Limited liability companies

- Pass through taxation.

- This type of business structure has no restrictions on the number of members required to be in the company.

- Members have the freedom to structure the management of their business how they please.

- This type of legal business structure has no formalities nor does it require certain paperwork like corporations.

- The owners of the business are not liable for debts and losses the business incurs.

- The profits and losses of the business are passed through the company to every member.

Disadvantages of limited liability companies

- They have a limited life.

- They are more expensive to start compared to general partnerships and sole proprietorship businesses.

- The ownership of the business is hard to transfer compared to that of a corporation.

Step 3: Take care of the legal requirements

When it comes to the law, there are a few requirements that every freight brokerage business must adhere to. Some of the most essential legal requirements include:

An operating authority: As I mentioned earlier, for a Freight Brokerage Company to operate, it requires an operating authority from the Federal Motor Carrier Safety Administration. The Federal Motor Carrier Safety Administration is a government body that regulates interstate commerce. It also enforces safety rules in the freight industry. You are required to pay an application fee of $300 and the operating authority can take approximately four to six weeks to receive approval.

An insurance cover: An insurance cover is also an essential requirement for anyone looking to start a freight brokerage business. Some of the insurance coverages you require include liability insurance and cargo insurance. All of which require you to make down payments of approximately 20% to 30% and premium payments as well.

A complete unified carrier registration: You have to acquire a complete unified carrier registration and then pay an annual fee that is currently at $76.

Abide by local and state requirements: Every state and local government has laws that govern the operation of freight brokerage businesses within their jurisdiction. Therefore, ensure that you check your local and state government for any other requirements that will enable you to operate your freight brokerage business within your state.

Follow recordkeeping requirements: It is a requirement for freight brokers to keep accurate records of all their business orders for each transaction done for three years. You will also be required to make these records available to all parties. The records of all your transactions should include:

- Shipper's address and name

- Carrier's address, name, and registration number

- Bill of landing

- Your rates and the name of the client that paid for your services

- Other services you performed that were not freight broker related, how much those services cost, and the person that settled the obligation

- The date the carrier was paid and the freight charges you collected

Step 4: Designate a process agent

In the previous chapter, we looked at the process of acquiring a process agent. Just a small reminder, a process agent is your representative when it comes to court cases. The court serves them your court case papers and they act on behalf of a freight broker in legal proceedings. A freight broker is required to have a process agent in every state their business operates in. However, freight businesses opt to have one company that oversees all the legal proceeding in every state.

When choosing a blanket company to act as your process agent, ensure you choose a company that is trusted and reputable. You can also look for referrals from other freight broker companies, as they will honestly tell you the right blanket company to designate as a process agent.

Step 5: Arrange to acquire a trust fund or surety bond

Once you designate a process agent, the next step is arranging to place a surety bond. Surety bonds are put in place to ensure that your customers are compensated when you break the contract. It also keeps you from practicing unlawful business practices. It also protects carriers and shippers from fraudulent acts by freight brokerage businesses.

As mentioned earlier, the current amount freight brokers are required to produce for their surety bond is $75,000. This is a huge amount to put up as surety especially for a businessperson just joining the freight industry so make sure you don't break the law. Only serious businesspeople are able to put up such a large amount into a surety bond.

However, you are not required to pay the full amount upfront. You can pay that amount in a certain period using the help of an insurance company.

The payment of the surety bond has helped sift out unlawful freight brokers from starting a business. To acquire help paying for the surety bond, a majority of banks and investors look at your credit.

Therefore, ensure that you have exemplary credit before you go looking for funds to pay the trust fund. Bad credit can be a huge obstacle for people looking for additional funding.

Step 6: Check the requirements of your state

Before you even set up your business, ensure that you check the requirements of your state when it comes to starting and operating a freight brokerage business.

Step7: Set up your office

Once you have checked the requirements of your state when it comes to starting a freight business, the next step is setting up your office. As a new business, you can choose to set up your office at home or in a commercial space. Your office will also require operation equipment like a computer, a phone, and a fax machine.

Make sure to include recurring costs like taxes, insurance, internet and phone charges, utilities, rent if you are using a commercial space, payroll if you have employees, and a subscription fee for transportation management software among other expenses.

Your office presentation is crucial mainly because it is the face of your business. Ensure that you have a visible website that will make it easy for clients to learn about your business and the services you offer that set you apart from other freight brokers in the industry. In addition, try to integrate technology in the running process of your business, as this will make you more efficient.

Step 8: Get broker paperwork and contracts

Once you set up your office, consider yourself ready to start conducting business. Documents are a requirement in the freight broker industry; therefore, ensure that you get the relevant broker contracts needed for you to operate your business. Some of the contracts include the bill of landing, carrier qualifications, receivables, payables, and many more.

Step 9: Find carriers

Identifying carriers that are qualified and willing to transport freight is a crucial step since it determines the success of your business. Here are some tips you can use to help you locate professional, skilled, and qualified carriers for your business.

- Referrals: One of the most efficient ways of finding the right carriers for your business is through referrals. Established freight businesses can advise you accordingly on a carrier company that is reliable and trustworthy when it comes to the transportation of freight.

- Use load boards: You can also use load boards. There are free and paid websites that can give you access to over 100,000 carriers for you to choose from. The diversity of carriers on this site enables you to have a huge selection of carriers for you to choose from. A load board is normally hosted online and specific users are required to pay a subscription fee for them to log in. After logging in, one can post loads or empty trucks for them to cover their freight or have their trucks loaded. The load board is responsible for facilitating communication among the broker, shipper and owner or small carrier. Additionally, load boards are not just freight marketplaces but they can offer more. For instance, certain websites offer users with accurate data in the load board for a better experience when matching freight.

Step 10: Find shippers

Once you find carriers, next you have to find shippers. After all, they are the backbone of your business and without them, it becomes impossible for you to make an earning from your business. However, finding shippers is sometimes a challenging task. Therefore, here are a few tips to help you locate shippers.

Look at your competition: One of the best places for you to start looking for shippers is by observing your competition. Every product that other freight brokers transport has a source. Therefore, try to look into who the manufacturers of that product are then use that information to find out its competitors. You get insight into that company by simply keeping industry peer tabs.

Review your personal purchase history: Another way you can find shippers is through reviewing your purchase history. It does not matter whether it is receipts or your online order history; the products you order have manufacturers and are transported from somewhere. Therefore, get creative with the information you acquire from your search results. Understand how the company is connected, look for information that can lead you to the manufacturer, and do not give up - the possibilities are limitless.

Look around: Look around you, the things you see are most likely hauled no matter where you are. The clothes you wear, the pens in your office, or the furniture in your house; there is a likely possibility that 75% of those things were hauled. You can use that information to look for shippers for your business.

Use a shippers list: Look at an industrial directory to help you find shipping companies. You can search through such a directory using products, the name, or also look up detailed information about various shippers.

Step 11: Set your prices

The second to last step when starting your freight brokerage business is setting up your prices. You have to determine the price for each load. You can do this with the help of software such as a rate benchmarking software. This software helps freight brokers see the current prices for the spot freight market and the contracts.

Step 12: Move freight

Last but certainly not least you can finally start moving freight.

Chapter Summary

Setting up a freight brokerage business involves 12 steps. Each step has a requirement but the most essential steps are acquiring surety bonds, adhering to your local and state government, and acquiring operating authority.

Chapter Four: Common Problems You Will Face and How To Overcome Them

It is no secret that starting a business comes with its challenges. Sometimes, these challenges have been known to discourage business people as they begin or grow their businesses.

In this chapter, we are going to discuss the common problems you will face as you start and grow your freight business, and how to overcome them. Once you learn the type of difficulties to expect in the freight brokerage business, it becomes quite easy to tackle and handle them without getting discouraged.

1. Payment delay

One of the issues that plenty of start-up freight businesses face is payment delay, and this can sometimes be a problem especially for your carriers. In the freight broker industry, it is expected that the freight broker should pay his carriers long before the shipper pays for the goods transported by the freight broker. However, this can be quite a disadvantage to a business that has a limited cash flow.

This is what start-up freight brokerage businesses call a cash killer. The reason for this is that a majority of freight brokerage businesses often raid their reserve funds to cover the carrier payments. On the other hand, a freight broker has to wait approximately two to three weeks or even longer to receive their pay from the shippers.

Solution

If you want to grow your freight brokerage business, then consider shortening your payment clock. The first step you can use to reduce your payment clock is asking for an advance payment from your shipping company. This is one approach you can use to solve your finance issues. However, this approach can cause tension and disruptions with your customers down the road.

Another option is factoring. Freight brokerage factoring is a method that allows freight brokerage businesses to ensure they have enough cash on hand to pay their carriers and cover the expenses of their companies. Rather than delay your carriers or wait for shippers to delay your payment and then start stressing over the bills you have, freight brokerage factoring businesses can offer you the funds you require to grow your business.

How does factoring work?

Factoring enables freight broker companies to cover their business costs and pay their carriers immediately instead of waiting for approximately one month or three months to receive payment for services rendered. The factoring process is one that requires a freight brokerage factoring company to purchase unpaid freight bills, and they advance freight broker companies approximately 98% of the cash within 24 hours.

Factoring companies then collect your business payments from clients on the terms you set during the factoring agreement, and you continue conducting your business as usual. The process requires you to:

- Book and dispatch a load as usual

- Send that invoice to the freight brokerage factoring business

- Then the freight brokerage factoring company pays you and your carriers within 24 hours

Benefits of freight brokerage factoring

The main advantage of freight brokerage factoring is that it is able to bridge the financial gap between a freight broker, a carrier, and a shipper. A factoring business is able to provide a freight brokerage business with the funds it requires to pay its carriers and receive payment without having to wait months for shippers to release payment.

Another major benefit of freight brokerage factoring is that you acquire an alternative source of funding regardless of your collateral or personal credit score. Freight brokerage factoring companies usually study your payment history and creditworthiness and not your credit history.

If your business has never qualified for a loan before, you can be sure that your business can still be eligible for factoring funds depending on the work you get and the loyalty of your customers.

You can also use the opportunity of freight factoring to improve your business credit rankings and infuse the amount of money you receive to pay your expenses and carriers.

2. Building and maintaining customer and carrier relations

A majority of start-up freight brokers tend to only bid for jobs on specific lanes or freights only when they know that their business has a competitive advantage over other freight brokerage businesses when it comes to coverage and/or pricing. This behavior can limit the growth of your business. It is also a challenge freight businesses experience when they are first starting out.

Solution

The success of any business is dependent on the ability of your company to maintain relations with clients. The same applies to a freight brokerage business. You cannot grow your business if you do not learn how to build and maintain your freight brokerage business. As a freight broker, you are also expected to strengthen the relationships you have with your carriers. How exactly do you build and maintain your customer relations?

- <u>Stay relevant</u>: Businesses that know how to stay

relevant currently are able to build and sustain relationships with their customers. Staying relevant means that you have to advertise your business, create a good website, provide your customers with content like blog material, and engage with them on social media platforms.

Freight brokerage businesses that have a strong digital presence increase their opportunities of expanding their carrier and customer base. Using social media platforms, you can keep track of your marketing techniques. This helps you concentrate on marketing techniques that work and discard methods that do not work.

- Utilize technology: Make the most of technology and embrace the technology changes that can help you expand your carrier and customer base. For instance, you can encourage your customers to use an application like GPS tracking on their smartphones to track the progress of their goods. You can also use apps that help to track fuel efficiency or you can use delivery logs. Such applications enable your customers to trust the quality of your business, and at the same time, build relationships with them.

- Build loyalty and trust: Loyalty and trust are some of the factors that form the foundation of a business. As a freight broker, trust and loyalty are among the aspects you should develop with your carriers and customers. Without these, it becomes impossible for you to build and maintain your customers and carriers.

Loyalty improves relationships. It can also sometimes help you save money when it comes to the carriers you use. For instance, it can be quite tempting for a start-up freight brokerage business to opt for the cheaper carriers to increase profits; however, if their services are poor, this can lead to the loss of your business in the long run.

One of the ways you can build loyalty and trust between you and your customers is to reach out during the year but not ask for business directly. For instance, you can send items like cards or small tokens that show you appreciate your customers. It is a simple gesture, but it can go a long way in ensuring that your customers trust your services and business.

- Be transparent: If you make promises, keep them. The reason why a majority of carriers and customers do not trust freight brokerage businesses that are just starting out is because of their inability to keep their word. Remember, a promise is also a binding contract, which when broken it ends up ruining the trust your carriers and customers have in you and your business. If you are not able to keep your promise, then communicate this with them.

Transparency in business enables your customers and carriers to see things in your perspective. It also makes it easy to communicate as to why you will not be able to keep your promise. The more you communicate with your carriers and customers, the easier it becomes to build and maintain a relationship with them.

- Listen to your customers and carriers: Listening is vital in building and maintaining any relationship. It does not matter whether you are asking your friends about their day or receiving an order from a client, you have to listen. Starting a freight brokerage business requires you to ask questions and listen to the answers your clients and carriers give you. For instance, some of the questions you might ask your carriers could be things such as; what lanes do they prefer? What weights do they haul?

For your customers, other questions you should ask include; what services do they prefer? What is their budget for a particular shipment? In addition to listening to the answers your clients give you concerning the questions you raise, you should also strive to listen to their suggestions and comments about your business.

- Offer your customers value-added services: If you want your business to stand apart from other companies, you can try developing a capacity sourcing strategy that will make it easy for your customers and carriers to trust your business. Offering your customers value-added services is one way to ensure you keep building and maintaining your relationships.

3. Redundant overheads

Freight brokerage businesses that are already established often have dispatch centers that are overcrowded with staff working emails, phones, and fax machines. This can prove to be a challenge for freight brokerage businesses since much of the time your staff works will be spent confirming load acceptance, handling quotes, making calls, and locating freight. Having excessive staff can also make it quite difficult for you to manage your finances due to the expenses you have to incur.

Solution

You can opt to scale down your staff and use technology. Technology is advancing every day making it easy for businesses to reduce redundant overheads. You can use new technology designed to help you automate the numerous tasks your business has daily. You can use this new technology to dispatch teams, check delivery logs, track freight, and have in-house tracking.

4. Damage claims or cargo loss

It is important to realize that as a freight broker damage claims or cargo loss is something that is bound to happen if you stay in the business long enough. This can be a difficult thing to deal with. You'll have to explain to the customer that their cargo was lost and that can be a difficult conversation to have. Damage claims and cargo loss can also run you out of business if you're not properly prepared. So what should you do to set up the best possible defense against damage claims or cargo loss?

Solution

The first step is to ensure that you understand the entire process of dealing with damage claims and loss of cargo. This information is essential as it helps you deal with such cases when they arise.

The next step is to make sure that you have the proper

insurance to cover any type of damage claim or cargo loss claim that might occur. It might seem like a hassle to have to pay for something that you hope you never use.

However if an accident does occur, you'll be glad that you have insurance. Insurance can make the difference between continuing to run your business smoothly and having to shut things down.

It'll also help to give you peace of mind knowing that if something bad were to happen you'd at least be covered. As far as explaining what happened to your clients in the case of cargo loss, this can be a bit tricky.

What you don't want to do is put the blame on someone or something else. Make sure you own up to it and take responsibility even though you probably weren't the person who directly caused the loss to happen.

Then explain to them how you'll replace the monetary value of what the goods were worth. It does you no good to take responsibility only to not be willing to pay the cost of the lost goods.

The reason why you want to do this is because it builds trust between you and the customer. The customer will know that you're reliable and can be depended upon if something does go wrong. That will go a long way in this industry.

Encountering challenges in business is part of the entrepreneurship experience. It causes you to think outside the box and come up with viable solutions that help you and your staff grow the business. Therefore, whatever challenges you experience in the freight broker industry; remember there is always a solution.

Chapter Summary

- Some of the common problems freight brokerage businesses experience include redundant overheads, building and maintaining relationships with carriers and customers, and payment delays. Each of these problems have solutions.

- The solution to building and maintaining relationships includes building loyalty and trust, transparency, staying relevant, using technology and listening.

- Solving the problems you experience in the freight industry is one of the ways you grow your business and help your staff grow their skills in the freight industry as well.

Chapter Five: How To Scale Up Your Business To Multiple Six and Seven Figures

The success of any business is measured by the number of profits it earns at the end of every year. Sadly, the majority of business owners have chosen to accept the same profits each year. This should not be the case. Freight brokerage businesses have the capacity of producing six to seven figure profits only if you scale up your business.

In this chapter, we'll discuss strategies you can use to scale up your business. We will also look at how things change as your freight brokerage business grows and the new challenges you can expect along the way.

Strategies to help scale up your business

1. Integrate and automate

The one limitation a majority of start-up freight brokerage businesses have over already established businesses is that they tend to rely on paper-based offices to run their businesses. This means that your business is not scalable. Thanks to technology, it has become easier for companies to do away with paper-based offices and turn to technology.

Technology makes it possible for small freight brokers to increase their efficiency and capacity. It allows businesses to integrate technology in the services they offer clients, thus making it more useful for their customers to see what they do as a company. Freight businesses that fail to incorporate technology are merely falling behind, and this can lead to the closure of business in the long run.

Integrating technology helps you expand your customer base and this, in turn, leads to you growing your customer base. The more customers you attract, the higher the profit your business earns. You also get to connect with shippers and carriers ensuring that shipments arrive at their destinations on time without any delays.

2. Marketing

Another strategy that can help you scale up your business is the use of marketing. When marketing is done right, you can be sure that your business will be well on its way to earning six to seven-figure profits.

Not only does your company need to attract the right customers; you also need to attract the right shippers and carriers for your business. Marketing plays an integral role in ensuring that you reach the right customers and find honest shippers and brokers. Therefore, how do you market your business?

- List your business in business directories: The first thing a majority of customers, shippers, and carriers do when looking for a freight broker is visit the

Internet. Using the Internet, they can come up with a list of freight brokerage businesses that can offer them the services they require. List your business in business directories that are on the Internet and use local directories in your city as well.

- Find leads online: Instead of waiting for clients to come to you, you can choose to go to them. Established freight brokerage businesses are always looking for prospective clients that require their services, and this puts them at the top of other freight broker companies. You can also do the same for the carriers you use.

- Use content creation: Another marketing strategy you can use to scale up your business is content creation. Creating content about the freight broker industry helps you connect to your customers. It also enables them to learn more about your business from the content you write.

- Create a website: Clients want to see an online presence before they can acquire your services. Clients often avoid companies that do not have legitimate websites, meaning that if your site is not as professional as it should be, then you are losing plenty of clients in the process.

Ensure that your website has comprehensive details of everything about your company, your services, your capabilities, and contacts. It would also be an added bonus if you included several client testimonials of your services. Client testimonials are in a way a reflection of the efficiency and quality of your services.

3. Networking

Surviving in business on your own can be tough; that's why it's important to get help from other people and businesses in your industry wherever and whenever you can. Networking is also another strategy you can use to scale up your business. Networking is your ability to interact with individuals or other companies and engage with them. It helps you grow your business thanks to the advice you acquire from established, prosperous companies.

You can also use networking as a tool that will enable you to acquire business investors that can inject the right amount of capital for you to scale up your business. Some of the ways you can network are through face-to-face appearances such as conferences, events, or business negotiations.

You can also use social media platforms as well. The more you network, the more you learn, and the more your business will grow. Networking is essential nowadays.

4. Hire the right people

Another critical influence on the success of your business is the staff. If you hire staff that is not skilled at what they do, then you can be sure your business will not grow.

Ensure that the team you hire while developing your company are efficient, skilled, and great at what they do. Do not just hire staff to increase your headcount, hire staff that will help you grow your business. Some of the factors you should consider when hiring staff include:

- Experience: Experience in the freight broker industry

is essential for the staff you employ, as you require them to know the ins and outs of the industry. The experience they have will also make it possible to not spend too much time explaining what the responsibilities are that come with the job.

- Personality: Since the freight broker industry deals a lot with people, you should hire people who are friendly and welcoming to your clients. You would not want to drive your customers away because of a bad attitude from one of your staff members.

You can also opt to train new yet enthusiastic employees as to how you run your business.

New challenges to expect as your business grows

Every new freight brokerage business experiences challenges and changes as the business starts to grow. However, the challenges you experience will depend on your background and experience in the freight industry. If you have worked in the freight broker industry before, you will have a better understanding of the freight industry.

Despite the challenges you'll face, it is essential for you to realize that starting a freight brokerage business is quite rewarding and at the same time challenging. So here are some of the new challenges you can expect and the solutions to these issues.

The first challenge a majority of new freight brokerage

businesses experience during the first year of business is that very few carriers are ready to work with you. Carriers are hesitant to work with start-up freight brokerage businesses because they are new in the industry and do not have published credit.

One of the ways you can solve this issue is through establishing a connection with trucking companies before you start your business.

You require carriers to help you move freight and establishing a connection with carriers before you start your business is one way to ensure that you do not lack transporters along the way.

Another challenge first-year freight businesses experience is the lack of shippers. The reason for this - well you guessed it - is that your business is new.

Shippers often frown upon the thought of working with new companies because they have no way of proving that your business is reliable. This is because your business does not have a history of freight delivery. From an accountability standpoint, shippers are often paranoid giving freight to companies they know little about.

You can avoid this problem by contacting shippers ahead of time. It also helps if you explain your experience beforehand to shipping companies as this helps them trust that you can deliver freight on time. Despite the resistance, a majority of shippers don't mind working with new freight businesses as much as they are still open to working with experienced freight brokers.

Insurance payments are another issue that affects new brokerage businesses. Obtaining an insurance policy is an easy process but making payments can be quite challenging for freight brokerage businesses in their first year. You might be able to write a check and clear the first year premium payment, but not every freight brokerage business can afford to make that payment year after year.

As I mentioned earlier, most insurance companies require freight brokerage businesses to make down payments of approximately 20% to 30% before they can qualify for the coverage that they need. If you have bad credit, then this can be a problem for you. For start-up businesses, the 20% to 30% down payment can be quite costly, and this pushes some people to start their business later. It also drives some people willing to start freight brokerage businesses totally away causing them to look for other businesses with fewer expenses they can start.

A majority of start-up freight brokerage businesses often opt to start their businesses by using spreadsheets to document everything about their business. This can, however, be quite limiting and overwhelming for businesses that have over 10 to 15 loads. Having a software program makes it easy for you to plan your business and figure out how things should operate during the first year of business.

Financing is also a challenge during the first year of business. Once you ship freight, your carriers also require payment before they can transport the cargo for you.

What happens when you do not have any capital to pay your carriers? Well, the first year of any freight business is faced with such challenges, and the best solution is freight factoring.

We discussed freight factoring in chapter 4, so you can re-read that chapter to find out more about freight factoring.

Before you even acquire the services of a factoring company, ensure that you do your homework because the factoring company you trust to fund your business can either make or break it.

Once you cross the first year threshold and overcome all the above challenges, then you should congratulate yourself. A majority of start-up freight brokerage businesses do not last that long, and they end up giving up along the way.

For your freight broker business to survive, you need to move freight constantly, or you are more than likely going to go out of business. You also require efficient operations and dispatch services.

Without these three factors, it becomes impossible to make profits, and this eventually runs your business to the ground. Once your business makes it out of the first year, some of the new challenges you experience are:

Margin preservation: This is one of the challenges a business running past one-year experiences. For businesses that have been running for approximately 18 months, they often tend to come under scrutiny from an outgoing traffic manager. In addition, corporations can also interfere with the daily running of your business primarily because of the rates you offer. To avoid this, ensure that you adhere to every requirement the government wants you to follow.

The expansion of your customer base: After operating for almost a year, a majority of freight brokerage businesses often get stuck in a rut that causes them not to expand their customer base. One way of dealing with this problem is through networking and marketing.

Whatever the problems you experience, remember that these

challenges are there to help you learn how to grow your business, enable you to take risks and think outside the box to obtain solutions to the problems your business is experiencing.

Chapter Summary

- Your first year as a freight broker has certain challenges that cause the majority of businesses to not survive, as they are not able to acquire solutions to these challenges.

- Some of the challenges first-year businesses experience are insurance payments, lack of carriers and shippers, and lack of funds. The good news is that each of these challenges have their solutions. Some might require more creativity to solve than others, but nonetheless it's still possible to overcome seemingly difficult problems.

Chapter Six: How To Negotiate

Your Way To a Thriving Business

Negotiation is a crucial part of the freight brokerage business. Learning how to go about negotiating with your clients, shippers, and carriers is one of the ways you can ensure your business grows.

In this chapter, we are going to talk about the importance of negotiation in the freight brokerage business. We will also look at tips that will help you become a good negotiator and some of the common mistakes that people make during negotiations that can make them lose their businesses.

- It builds respect: Respect is an important aspect of any business. Without respect, it becomes extremely difficult for you to build lasting relationships with your clients, carriers, and shippers. It's also important for your team as this is key when it comes to improving their productivity. Your negotiation skills can either make or break the respect your team, clients, shippers, and carriers have for you.

The impression you leave people with after a negotiation leaves a lasting impression that can impact your business, future negotiations, and your reputation in the freight broker industry. When it comes to negotiations, you want to be firm and confident, you don't want to come across as a pushover. This will help in building respect and maintaining relationships with your shippers, clients, employees, and carriers.

- <u>You create win-win situations:</u> Contrary to popular belief, negotiations are not about winning over other parties; they are about coming into an amicable solution for all parties. There is truly no point of negotiating if your primary intention is to ensure you come out on top. Win-win negotiations explore both positions and come up with mutually acceptable outcomes that offer both parties what they want.

Negotiations in the freight industry can quite often create win-win situations for all parties if handled correctly. So, how can you create a win-win situation for your business and other parties during negotiations?

First, separate the people involved in the negotiations from the problem. Avoiding to identify negotiating parties with the problem helps you ignore your differences, and focus on the real problem at hand.

It helps you see things from your opponents' perspective and arrive at a deal that is fair, reasonable, and beneficial for both parties. Secondly, focus on the interests of both parties and not the positions. Once you choose to focus on the interests of all parties involved in the negotiations and not the positions, it becomes quite easy for all parties to come up with a solution despite the position of the company.

The best negotiators in any business are the people who create win-win situations for all the parties involved in the negotiations.

- <u>Build relationships:</u> The process of negotiation is one of the methods you can use to build relationships with stakeholders in your company. An excellent negotiator understands that negotiations are not only done in closed rooms, they are also done outside the negotiating room. Building a relationship with the negotiating party before negotiations start enable you to build relationships and maintain them.

Tips to help you become an excellent negotiator

Listen: An exceptional negotiator knows how to keep quiet and listen to the other side when they are talking. They are like detectives probing the other negotiating party with questions and then keeping quiet to listen to their response. In business, listening can solve so many quarrels. The more you listen, the easier it becomes for you to determine what the other party requires from you.

Do your homework: Before entering a negotiating room, do your homework. It helps when you come fully prepared to discuss a particular issue once you learn more about it. You are able to identify the options you have, what the needs of the other party are, and what pressures both parties have been experiencing concerning the issue at hand.

Doing your homework prior to negotiations increases the chances of success. You also make accurate decisions based on what you found out about the other party. You can also come up with a win-win situation for both parties much easier if you do your research in advance. More often than not, being able to come up with a winning solution comes down to how prepared you are before the negotiation even starts.

Chapter Summary

- Negotiating is a skill and the more you develop it, the easier it becomes for you to exercise it.

- Some of the ways you can develop your negotiating skills is through doing your homework, learning to listen, and finding out more about the other party. Sharpening your negotiating skills in business makes it possible for you to succeed in the freight brokerage business.

- One major benefit of improving your negotiating skills is building relationships. Your negotiating skills can make or break your business relationships. Therefore, ensure that you improve them, as this will help you build and maintain relationships without having to work extremely hard to do so.

Chapter Seven: Characteristics of a Successful Freight Broker

Becoming a successful freight broker does not only mean that you are experienced in this field, but you also contain the characteristics that successful freight brokers have. Success is not defined by the amount of profit your business makes or the amount of money you have in a bank account, but by the positive impact you cause in your surroundings.

In this chapter, we will talk about the characteristics of a successful freight broker. This will help you prepare the grounds for yourself as you start your freight brokerage business.

Characteristics of successful freight brokers

1. Trustworthiness and honesty

I cannot stop stating how important trust and honesty are in the business world. Without these two factors from the very beginning of your business, it becomes tough for you to maintain relationships let alone create them. A freight broker that is honest and trustworthy always attains results even when the odds are against him/her. The clients trust that you will consistently deliver even when there are challenges along the way.

Being honest at all times ensures that you are also transparent when you are communicating with shippers and carriers. The more transparent you become, the easier it is for you to build trust with everyone around you.

Trustworthiness comes as a result of being honest. When you are honest about the conditions of freight or about what you can and cannot do as a freight broker, it makes it easy for you not to make your clients empty promises. Consequently, freight brokerage businesses that only think of themselves have more to lose than companies that are honest with their clients from the very start.

2. Resilience

We all know that no business in the world is devoid of challenges and failures. Any successful freight broker can tell you that they once felt like giving up because of the difficulties they have faced while in the freight brokerage business. However, what sets them apart from other freight brokerage businesses that gave up shortly after starting is the resilience they had.

Resilience is your ability to bounce back and adapt even in the face of unexpected challenges. It is the ability to know when to not give up or give in to the problems your business is going through.

What makes resilience an essential characteristic for freight brokers to have?

- Resilience helps you develop mechanisms, which you

can use for protection against overwhelming experiences in business.

- It helps you learn how to create a balance in your life during those stressful and challenging moments as you run your business.

- It keeps you from developing mental health issues such as anxiety due to the problems you face.

Successful freight brokers are not easily rattled by challenges; they can keep calm, make decisions, come up with possible solutions, and make their customers happy even when the odds are against them.

3. Flexibility

Flexibility is another significant characteristic almost every freight broker should learn to develop. Flexibility is important as it enables you to make decisions even when you are up against a wall concerning a particular order.

You can shift things around on behalf of your clients, rearrange your loads, and make your clients happy with the decisions you make on their behalf.

Flexibility makes it easy for freight brokers to deliver quality even when they are faced with tough challenges. It makes them not succumb to the chaos and focus on the goals they have for their business.

4. Self-motivation

Successful freight brokers are driven by a passion for ensuring that their businesses grow despite the challenges they face. They have a reason to keep pushing on even when the job becomes quite monotonous.

This is what we call self-motivation. Whether it's perfection, time, money, family, or acquiring enough finances to start a particular project, whatever the reason, they are able to wake up early in the morning and get going. The reason for their motivation is what gets them through the entire day.

Surprisingly, the motivation that successful freight brokers have is not always driven by the amount of money they make; sometimes it is purely an inner drive that makes them want to see the job done in the right way using the appropriate methods. They are efficient at what they do, and this enables them to build a relationship with customers, shippers, and carriers.

Even when their businesses are slow and not generating plenty of profit; you will still find them ready to get to work. Business people in general who have no self-motivation, often struggle to keep their businesses afloat due to the lack of passion and pride that is needed in order to succeed. This makes it easy for them to throw in the towel when faced with challenges.

5. Customer oriented

A successful freight broker understands that his/her business cannot run if his/her customers are unhappy.

Therefore, a successful broker will make his/her business customer centered.

After all, a satisfied and happy customer will always be loyal. Successful freight brokers understand the value their customers have in their business, and they make it their mission to satisfy their every requirement.

They are devoted to their customers' interests, and this makes it possible for them to grow their business. In this case, it involves the shipper's interest to see their freight safely delivered and done on time.

A deep sense of customer focus makes it easy for freight brokers to earn referrals bringing in other customers without having to go out looking for them. The more your business focuses on its clients, the easier it becomes to build and maintain a long-term relationship with all your clients.

Therefore, if your company is not customer oriented then try to incorporate methods that help you put your customers first and give them the opportunity to express their interests about your services.

6. They keep on learning

A successful freight broker does not stop learning about the freight industry; they regularly update their knowledge about the industry by learning the latest trends, and technology. When you dare to learn something different about the industry, you can come up with solutions to challenges that a majority of brokers may have not thought of in the beginning.

Learning regularly helps you anticipate change, innovations, and challenges without fear of the future. It also enables you to improve your skills tremendously, making you different from other freight brokers in the industry. You are also able to set apart truths and create a learning environment for the rest of your team.

Freight brokers who continuously improve their skills through learning are able to network, share what they learn with others, and encourage other freight brokers to continue increasing their knowledge about the freight industry.

In addition to the knowledge they gain, they are also able to grow and develop their business using strategies that are different from other freight brokers. If you want to learn the secret of growth and success, then continue learning. I can assure you it is completely worth it.

7. They have a strategic mindset

The daily routine of a freight broker involves plenty of details that require the attention of the broker. Dealing with these details can be an intensive affair, primarily because of the attention each detail requires. A majority of freight brokers tend to lose sight of their vision and the big picture behind their business; this can cause them to look at the amount of work that has to be done as torture and not as an advantage.

Having a negative attitude towards the amount of work you have to do in your business can cause you to make short-term decisions that will not help you in the long run. Such decisions end up affecting the performance of your business. Successful freight brokers have strategic mindsets that enable them to review their ideas, refine their work schedules, and continue learning more about the industry.

A strategic mindset enables freight brokers to also stay on top of issues that surround the freight industry. It also enables you to adapt to negative changes in the market without experiencing disappointments.

8. They are result driven

Successful freight brokers define their tactical actions and set goals. A majority of freight brokers often get stuck in the launch preparations of their businesses and often forget about the future of their businesses. They end up taking plenty of time crafting their business plan, perfecting their procedures and documents, studying the market, among other details and they end up forgetting to set goals and milestones they can use.

Successful freight brokers understand the importance of goal setting and this causes them to be result driven. They expect results from their employees and their business. They come up with ideas and then split those goals into milestones, which they strive to achieve within a certain time period. They work hard to ensure they achieve every goal they set despite the obstacles they face in the process.

Chapter Summary

- Some of the common characteristics that successful freight brokers have include honesty, trustworthiness, result driven, and a strategic mindset among others.

- Your characteristics as freight broker are what

determine the level of success you achieve in the freight brokerage business. The more you cultivate the above characteristics, the easier it becomes to practice them. Cultivating the above characteristics helps in ensuring that you get to achieve everything you set out to do when starting your freight brokerage business.

Conclusion

Each of the above chapters has detailed all the requirements you need to start your freight brokerage business and be successful. However, the decision to start the business has to start with you. I have given you the tools you require; it is now time for you to take those tools and use them to your advantage.

There are plenty of freight brokerage businesses that have managed to succeed even with limiting odds; you can also do the same. All you need is patience, perseverance, knowledge, and a guiding hand from freight brokers that have already gone ahead of you.

Therefore, do not waste time! Start drafting that business plan and make your freight brokerage business a reality and not just an idea.

Remember that becoming a successful freight broker does not only mean that you are experienced in this field, but that you also have the characteristics of a successful freight broker. Success is not solely defined by the amount of profit your business makes or by the amount of money you have in a bank account.

Success is also about the positive impact you cause in your surroundings. Therefore, ensure that you strive to start a business that will not only influence this generation but other generations to come.

You should also check with the authorities for you to know the requirements needed before venturing into this business. Laws, regulations and licenses may vary depending on the country you live in or plan to start the business in.

Another thing you need to do is always make sure that you have a plan and you're prepared. Take your time to plan and do a thorough market research before venturing into a freight brokerage business. If you fail to plan, you plan to fail.

Faith without action is also dead. No matter how much optimism you have in this business, make sure you follow the advice as well as steps highlighted within this book for you to realize success.

If you choose to start your business after reading this, be sure to make the most out of the opportunities you get and scale up your business to a level that you are happy with.